As I Tra
the Vall

An Awareness Documentary
The Dead Rely on the Living to Tell Their Story

Margaret Dawson Brown

Llumina
Press

Requests for permission to make copies of any part of this work should be mailed to Permissions Department, Llumina Press, 7970 NW 4th Place, Plantation, FL 33324.

ISBN:978-1-62550-535-4 (PB)

This documentary has been written as a roadmap to the wrongful death claim for my brother, James Dawson

It is meant to provide an understanding of God's will and his promises to us. We all will experience great pain, in the past, now, or in the future; we had to go through it. God has a divine purpose for us, and we have a destiny to fulfill. Once we overcome, we are better equipped to understand and pray for others.

Preface

Let the record show, this story is not about me. I am just the product of a very powerful seed planted inside me by my parents. Without the seed nurturing and strengthening me mentally, I could not have been the composer of such a personal documentary. I was the first-born of five children, and I have always taken my role as a big sister seriously and with pride. I have always kept a spirit of open communication with my family. The strong foundation with which the Dawson children were raised has enabled each of us to become successful, upstanding citizens. We were raised to believe we could conquer anything together. The strength in our family makes it all worth striving for.

To appreciate what we have, we must first realize *what* we have. Once that has been established, we will discover that a real family is the most precious gift anyone can have. We are all born into a family, but that is not enough. We must constantly apply ourselves and work for the positions we have been blessed to hold. From mothers to fathers, from sisters to brothers, we are the main ingredients in our families, and working as a family is what life is all about.

I have been blessed to have a mom who never had to leave us to go to work. Being a full- and overtime mom to her children is all she has ever known. Mom is pure gold, filled with understanding, support, inspirations, encouragements, and much more. Mom is the light to direct us, the food to nourish us, and the shield to protect us; Mom is simply remarkable.

I have been blessed to have a dad who always provided for his family. Dad worked hard and dedicated himself to his family. Dad instilled in his children responsibility and accountability. Dad and Mom have had a great impact on the lives of their children, which enabled us to be all we can be.

i

From the day we were born, love and inspiration was fed to us. Our parents are indeed our role models.

I graduated from Martin Luther King High School in 1977. I attended Catherine Scott Secretarial School and graduated in 1979. The United States Postal Service employed me since July 1979. Unfortunately, two years following my brother's untimely death, after the legal system failed my family, I had to quit my job to spend the time needed to investigate his demise and compile this documentary. After finalizing this documentary, my plans are to pursue a career studying law. It's ironic, because when I graduated high school, I received a scholarship to study law. I became a mother, so I put my dreams of studying law behind me. My priority was to be the best mother I could be and to provide for my child and myself. For the past twenty-five years, I have been successful. It is simply amazing, though. I would have never imagined my dream of studying law could resurface. After twenty-five years, the Lord assured me that it is never too late to follow my dreams, and my brother's death actually led me back to this destiny.

I also have always enjoyed expressing my feelings through writing, though even in writing, we must first be the reader. We must try to communicate successfully to other readers in the hopes that all parties receive the same message. So at this time, I must put the facts and my thoughts together to produce a most powerful message in this documentary. While compiling this documentary, I had to write everything down in longhand then later type it out on my typewriter. Unfortunately, I am not familiar with the computer world. Everything is computerized or computer-oriented. I graduated from secretarial school in 1979, and for the past twenty-three years, I have not had the opportunity to use my secretarial skills. I had to dig deep into my background and give this documentary my best shot. With a little computer knowledge, I could have eliminated all the white-out, all the thrown-away papers, all the ointment I've had to use on my wrists and arms, and all the Tylenol, and *Web-*

ster's Dictionary probably would not have became one of my best friends. I was not meant to take an easier route to compiling this documentary, I guess; nevertheless, I will become acquainted with the evolving computer world I am blessed to be a part of.

The truth of the matter is that through all of the pains I felt and tears I cried while compiling this documentary, this has been a therapeutic method of dealing with the tragic loss of my brother. Watching this documentary unfold and develop into a beautiful and enlightened novel dedicated to my brother's memory makes all my pains and tears worth going through. To know that the truth shall be known is what this documentary is all about, and I hope it will be enlightening and therapeutic to you as well.

I thank God for the strong and loving support of my family and friends, but I would especially like to thank God for my son. Had it not been for him traveling along with the family, witnessing James' death, and discovering so many clues, the journey I have been blessed to travel may have never taken place. I submitted fifty pages of incriminating evidence to substantiate our claim of a wrongful death to several attorneys, civil rights organizations, and other establishments, but that was not enough to get the attention needed to have somebody, anybody, step in and assist in our fight for justice. It is a cold world out there, and we cannot change it, but we do not have to let it change us. I refuse to let other's excuses override my efforts. I must shake their dust off my feet and move on. I must hold my head up and praise God, from whom all blessings flow. No one is immune to the trials of life, and my hard-learned lesson is "Sometimes we have to lose in order to win." If knowing the circumstances surrounding my brother's death may somehow save the lives of others by bringing awareness to an epidemic of alleged suicides while in police custody, his death has purpose. That is why I must tell his story. Not only the dead, but also the living, rely on me to deliver this story.

Introduction

The story you are about to read has been outlined in the order I feel is necessary to journey into James Dawson's death. Once you read this story, it does not matter what color you are; what really matters is that we are all first human beings and special to someone. Now sit back and imagine an ordeal of this nature. What would you have done if this tragedy had happened to you? It can happen to anyone and has already happened to many, so please, beware. You may also want to grab your rubber boots and put them on, because you are definitely going to need them. We have so much to step in as we travel through the valley of death.

When a loved one who has never had a brush with the law in the entire thirty-seven years of his life is one day traveling alone and stopped for speeding, only to be taken to jail because his license was suspended...

When this loved one has always been totally against suicide, but all of a sudden, seems to commit suicide while being detained in jail...

When the presentation of this loved one's death has this many holes in it and those whose fields of expertise are challenged, implicating them in a cover-up...

When we must face this situation without any justice to defend our suspicions or ourselves...

When we know in our hearts, in our minds, in our souls, what a loved one is made of, and someone tries to convince us otherwise...

It's a hard pill to swallow.

Then, once we are flooded with a preponderance of evidence, proving beyond any doubt what we had known all along, and nobody feels we have enough to substantiate our claim of a wrongful death, it's an even harder pill to swallow, but there's still hope, because sometimes we just have to raise our voices in order to be heard. Maybe one day, that voice will make a difference.

Main Characters

In memory of my brother   James Dawson (Pookie)
The author   Margaret (Dawson) Brown
The mother   Lillie Dawson
The nephew (my son)   Michael Brown
The brother   Stevie Dawson

The facility where James Dawson was taken to be detained after being caught driving on a suspended license—the Cumberland County Correctional Facility in Toledo, Illinois

The officer who initially discovered the body of James Dawson hanging from the shower curtain rod inside his holding cell and who saw him alive thirty minutes prior to the alleged hanging—Ms. Deborah Cornell

The hospital where James Dawson was pronounced dead upon arrival—the Sarah Bush Lincoln Health Center, located in Mattoon, Illinois.

The coroner of Coles County, Mr. Michael Nichols

The initial autopsy procedure was held at the Memorial Medical Center, located in Springfield and performed by Mr. Travis Hindman

The investigating officer assigned to the case, a special agent with the Illinois State Police Department, District # 9, from Effingham, Illinois, Mr. Kelly Hodge

The independent re-autopsy was held at the Evanston Northwestern Healthcare and performed by Mr. Michael Kaufman & Mr. Eugene Kouzov

The attorney who held the potential wrongful death claim for the family of James Dawson from November 2000 until March 2001, an associate with the Cochran, Cherry, Givens, Smith, and Montgomery L.L.C. of Chicago, Illinois, Mr. Douglas Hopson

The names have not been changed to protect anyone; I give you the actual characters and the roles they played in the death of James Dawson.

The Story

Was it a suicide or was it murder? How do we tell the difference? These are the questions asked in this documentary. Antagonists wish to confound us into believing James' death was self-inflicted; strong detective work is needed to prove otherwise.

This documentary contains evidence of covered-up crimes that occurred while James was detained in jail. I have never had experience with the jail system and never had to focus on its crimes before November 5, 2000, when my brother's vehicle was stopped for speeding. Death was the price he had to pay. When I think of jail, I think of those who have been sentenced and have to spend time there for a crime.

Unfortunately, my family was suddenly introduced to jailhouse crime when one of our own lost his life while being detained for a traffic violation. He was driving a few miles above the speed limit and his license was suspended, but he'd never had a criminal record. He had no warrants, no arrests—just a suspended license. This usually only took a couple of hours to straighten out. It usually resulted in a court date for the citation, not death!

I am not sure if detainment procedures for driving on a suspended license are the same in all areas, but I cannot believe it is just like a felony. You see, my brother was not just detained. He was arrested, booked, stripped of his clothes and personal belongings, issued a prison uniform, and processed as a prisoner within forty minutes of being stopped. It was not until I learned of all the suspicious circumstances surrounding his death that I discovered that many have lost their lives by hanging while being detained in jail. One can't help but wonder, "Have our jail houses turned into private lynching facilities?"

Although some hangings may be self-inflicted, some may also be committed by other prisoners or, believe it or not, members of the jail staff. When the jail staff are responsible for crimes either directly or by permitting them to occur, they must cover up what really happened. Some jails hire sadistic, brutish, racist monsters, giving them free rein to torture, rape, harass, and murder.

No matter how nice and normal a prison guard or administrator may appear, everyone who works for a prison has something to hide when faced with an unexpected death. I make this blanket condemnation because even those who do not participate in these crimes, by witnessing or having knowledge of a cover-up, and doing or saying nothing, are just as guilty. They find themselves with their backs against the wall. Being silent and blind appears to be the best medicine for keeping their jobs, and keeping the truth from being uncovered. They must stand behind that wall because anything else means disgracing themselves, their uniforms, and the city or town they are sworn to serve and protect. Unfortunately, the dead will be left with the evil of the silent and the blind.

When I think of suicide, my thoughts contain images of the extremely depressed, those incapable of handling what is going on in their lives. Suicide gets rid of the pain one is enduring. Whenever there are no signs of anything seriously wrong in a person's life, there will always be a question mark behind a suicide. When a family is presented with a suicide by a jail staff, what defense does the family really have? Even if a suicide note is written, who's to say it was written by choice? You don't expect anyone to admit they killed your loved one, do you? How is a family supposed to investigate a loved one's death when the proof lies in the hands of those working to protect their town and its jail staff by any means necessary? What about when the town coroner must provide proof of what really happened, and the coroner and all the individuals initially involved with the body are unable to identify any marks on the neck? However, all of them identify an abrasion on the chin—the exact same thing the victim's family witnessed and photographed. Can anybody tell me what is wrong with this picture?

Conveniently, once the victim's body was returned to the family after leaving the town coroner, it contained no internal organs, no tissue, no brain, and no blood. It was an empty cavity. How much more is really needed to provide proof that a cover-up has taken place? Naturally, if a wrongdoing can be revealed, there will be serious consequences and repercussions. Why not call the death a suicide, if possible?

Let us analyze this scenario. Let us take an employed African-American man who has worked every day of his life to prepare for better things. He is raising a teenage son, and every summer, during the break from school, his son accompanies him to work as he tries to instill in his child that life is what you make of it. This man has escaped the mercy of the streets and never had any brush with the law until this fateful night. This man is James Dawson.

After working double shifts for weeks, James received three days off together, so he and one of his close friends decided to travel to Tunica, Mississippi, to meet up with others and visit a well-known riverboat casino. James and his friend had traveled to Tunica on two other occasions and were very successful. They would only stay for one day and then head back to Chicago. On the evening they were supposed to leave, James' friend was called in to work, but James decided to go anyway. It was not uncommon for James to go wherever he wanted to go. He often traveled long distances alone, and he always had his cell phone with him.

On November 5, 2000, at approximately six p.m., James ate dinner with his family. Immediately following dinner, he headed out for his trip. At 11:20 p.m., the record shows James' vehicle was stopped for speeding on I-57 (southbound, just north of the Neoga exit, Post 179), two hundred miles from home. When the officer checked James' license, it came up suspended, and he was taken to the Cumberland County Correctional Facility for detainment.

The census showed that Cumberland County had a population of 11,253. This predominantly white area has 11,123 whites and 12 African-Americans; other nationalities make up the rest. On November 5, James was the only African-American being processed next to seven whites.

The official detention document shows that James was stripped of his clothes and personal belongings, issued a prison uniform, and processed as a prisoner. As I stated earlier, I'm not sure if detainment procedures for driving on a suspended license are the same in all areas, but to be processed as a prisoner without ever having a brush with the law seems unreal.

Nevertheless, at 2:17 a.m., over two hours after being processed, James finally got to call his family to let them know what had happened. He told Mom he did not know why his license was suspended and that they would not let him post his own bond. He needed someone to come to the jail to post bond. He told Mom the bond was set at $150, and then gave her directions to the jail. He even put the booking officer on the phone to confirm the directions. The officer gave James back the phone, and he and Mom continued making plans. James' tone was normal, and he even had a familiar chuckle in his voice as he talked to Mom. Although Mom did not drive, James knew preparations were being made, through the family, to get to him. You see, Mom had always had bad vibes about the police because years ago, her brother was badly beaten by them, so her son being in their hands was one of Mom's worst fears. Who in the world could have imagined her son would be dead when the family arrived?

At exactly eight a.m., immediately after mom sent the grandchildren off to school, the family headed for the Cumberland County jail. Due to bad rain, the three-hour trip turned into a three and a half-hour trip. The family arrived at the jail at 11:30 a.m. When Mom gave the clerk the $150 for her son's release, the clerk told Mom the amount due was only $100. Then the family was instructed to leave the facility and wait in their vehicle until James had been officially released. The clerk added that the release process would take about fifteen minutes and that James would come out the door where they had parked their vehicle. Returning to their vehicle in the rain, the family asked each other, "Why we couldn't just wait inside if the release process only took fifteen minutes? It's raining something terrible out here. How did the clerk know where we had parked?"

Was there a surveillance camera in the parking lot? The jail staff knew James Dawson's family would be arriving soon because Mom had talked to the officer in the booking area and told him that since the family was unfamiliar with the area and it was after two in the morning, they would be on their way as soon as daylight hit. Perhaps it is normal procedure to know where people have parked, but is it normal that those paying bail leave the facility and wait outside until their parties have been released? If this is not normal procedure for everyone, why was it necessary for James Dawson's family?

After waiting in their vehicle for almost forty-five minutes, Mom said to her son Stevie and grandson Michael, "This is the longest fifteen minutes I've ever seen."

Moments later, the clerk who instructed the family to leave the facility ran to their vehicle in the rain. "The release of your party will take a few minutes longer, due to a medical emergency."

No sooner than she explained the delay, an ambulance pulled up to the door of the jail. The ambulance department was located in the same area as the jail, practically within walking distance of one another. Anyway, the next thing you know, James is coming out of the door where the clerk said he would; however, he is being carried out on a stretcher, wearing only his underwear and socks, tubes sticking out of him.

Why did the clerk run all the way out to the family and intentionally withhold the most vital piece of information—that the medical emergency was actually for their party? Why say anything at all, especially if it was a lie? I feel that the clerk sent my family out of the facility to keep them from witnessing what was really going on in there. They had to set the scene up to make it look presentable, and I don't think they would have been comfortable doing this with my family sitting right there, watching everything. Instead, they sent the clerk to their vehicle to mislead them.

The family saw their party being carried out of the jail and into the ambulance. They immediately got out of their vehicle and ran over. James' hand was hanging off the stretcher. Mom grabbed her son's hand. It was cold as ice.

Mom screamed, "What happened to my son?"

The paramedics told the family to follow their ambulance to the local hospital. They followed the Toledo ambulance for about twenty minutes with no sirens, only flashing lights. The ambulance made a sudden stop a couple of minutes from the hospital, where another ambulance was waiting with its lights flashing. One of the paramedics transporting James got out of the ambulance to converse with the other. Michael got out of the family's vehicle to see what was going on. Moments later, the Toledo ambulance proceeded to the Sarah Bush Lincoln Health Center, where James was pronounced dead upon arrival. When have you ever seen an ambulance en route to the hospital during an emergency stop to converse with another?

The emergency room physician and a nurse taking notes stayed in the room with James for about ten minutes. Then the physician approached the family to inform them that James was dead. He allowed them to go into the room to be with the body. Michael asked if he could go first, alone, so he could spend a private moment with his uncle. Michael asked the emergency room physician, "How did my uncle die?"

The physician replied, "He hung himself."

"What did you say?"

The physician repeated, "I was told that he hung himself."

"What did he hang himself with?" asked Michael.

"I was told that a shower curtain was used."

"A shower curtain? This is crazy," said Michael as the physician walked away in sorrow.

When Michael held his uncle's head, he immediately noticed there were no marks on his neck. Michael screamed for Mom and Stevie to come into the room and pointed out to them what he had just observed. Michael said, "Take a look at Uncle Pookie's neck. If he hung himself, why aren't there any marks on his neck? The only thing here is an abrasion on his chin, which does not look as if it just happened. This abrasion is already brown, and it looks as if his chin was scraped against something. There are no marks on his neck. Do these people think that we are stupid or something because we are black?"

Michael stormed out of the room. Mom ran behind him and Stevie stayed inside the room. As soon as Mom knew Michael was okay, she went back to the room to continue viewing her son's body.

Michael had gone to the front desk to page the emergency physician because he left the room before Michael noticed the condition of the body. After waiting for some time, Michael was told that the emergency room physician was unavailable. Michael explained the situation to the desk clerk and described the nurse who was in the room taking notes, and he was directed to the nurse's station. Michael located the nurse and asked, "How did James Dawson die?"

The nurse replied, "He hung himself."

"What did he hang himself with?"

The nurse grabbed her notepad and read, "It says that he hung himself with a belt."

"A belt?" Michael responded. He had now been told of two different objects with which his uncle supposedly hung himself, and Michael was convinced that his uncle did not take his own life.

Michael asked the nurse if she could accompany him to the room where his uncle's body lay. She replied that she could, but she only had a few minutes to spare. Michael told the nurse that he was almost positive his uncle was not wearing a belt. When he was last seen, he was wearing a black jogging suit; however, when he was brought into the hospital, he was only wearing his underwear and socks. The nurse looked shocked. She then told Michael that she really did not have all the facts, but that someone would be assigned to the situation that would be better able to answer any questions he or the family may have.

Mom and Stevie had left the room and moved to the waiting area, awaiting a counselor and the coroner. Michael asked the nurse to look at his uncle's neck and tell him why, if he died from hanging, there were no marks on his neck.

The nurse looked at James' neck and said, "There is definitely something wrong here." Again, she explained that she did not have all the facts. Reassuring him that someone would be assigned to the situation, the nurse gave Michael her condolences and left. When the nurse left, Michael put up a terrible commotion, kicking the walls and screaming, "They killed my uncle," until Mom and Stevie had to restrain him. Mom was afraid Michael would be arrested for disorderly conduct or something, because the police were already at the hospital waiting for anything to jump off.

Stevie took Michael outside to calm down while Mom stayed inside to talk with the counselor and the coroner. Meanwhile, outside the hospital, Michael convinced Stevie to drive to the store to purchase a disposable camera and take photographs of James' neck. Upon their return, Michael apologized to everyone for the disturbance then asked if he and Stevie could view James' body one last time. Personnel escorted them back to the room. Michael went in the room alone and closed the door while Stevie stayed outside to distract the attendant. Michael took three photographs of James' body—both sides of the neck and the abrasion on the chin. Thereafter, Michael and Stevie were escorted to the waiting area where Mom was. Mom had already talked to the counselor, but she was only able to provide information given to her by the paramedics and the jail staff. On the other hand, the coroner had his own agenda. The coroner told Mom that, due to the nature in which her son died, it was the law that his body immediately be transported to Springfield for an autopsy. Mom told the coroner she would rather her son's body be transported to Chicago so that A.R. Leak's could handle everything. The coroner told Mom that was not possible. After Springfield completed their autopsy, Leak's could retrieve the body. No documents were signed, and no further information was given about the autopsy.

When the family returned to Chicago and Mom told me about her conversation with the coroner, I immediately called the hospital to ask whom I could talk to about the autopsy. I was given the name and number to the Office of the Coroner. I called the office, the coroner answered, and after I identified myself, I asked why, since the jail staff claimed to have witnessed James' hanging, that was not considered the cause of death. The coroner told me that the death occurred in his jurisdiction, so that gave him the authority to request an official determination by autopsy. I asked if I could attend the autopsy. He told me no one was allowed to attend the autopsy and that once the autopsy was completed, someone would contact the family. He made it perfectly clear that my family's rights did not override his decision for the autopsy. I asked why there were no marks on James' neck. The coroner evaded the question and told me he was very busy; however, everything would be documented on the autopsy report. That ended our conversation. My investigation revealed that family members do not have the right to refuse a coronial postmortem; it can be done regardless of the family's wishes. Therefore, when the coroner took possession of James' body, the secret of James' death was in his hands.

After leaving the hospital, the family was escorted back to the jail to pick up James' personal belongings. Mom requested a refund for the money she had just paid, and the money was returned. Michael asked if the family could see the holding cell James occupied, and his request was denied. The investigating officer arrived on the scene at the jail and when he heard the family was there, he immediately took Mom to a room and started asking personal questions about her son—more like an interrogation. Mom answered most of his questions, and then Michael stepped in and told the officer that if he had any more questions, he could contact our attorney. Although we did not have an attorney at the time, Michael did the right thing because the investigating officer then told the family that there is no need to contact their attorney because these people were his friends and he could assure them there was no foul play involved.

That comment alone should have been more than enough cause to put somebody else on this case. An investigating officer is supposed to be unbiased, but when he is in a position where his friends' livelihoods are on the line against the death of an African-American man, will justice truly be served? Unfortunately not.

Mom was given a clear plastic bag that contained all of James' personal belongings, including a sealed yellow envelope that supposedly contained the currency James had in his possession. The family was escorted to Dale's Amoco gas station, where James' vehicle was impounded. It was the only vehicle on the entire lot. A payment of $50 was needed to retrieve the vehicle. I guess that was why James told Mom the bond was set at $150.

When Michael got in the vehicle to drive back to Chicago, Mom asked if he needed to gas up. Michael noticed the gas gauge was past the full mark, so James must have filled his tank right before he was stopped for the traffic violation. The trip back to Chicago after the death of their loved one will be embedded in the minds of these three family members forever. But, you see, the blessing came when Michael rode along with Mom and Stevie because the Lord already had plans for his presence.

Dale's Amoco receipt that was given to Mom

Michael took the initiative in asking questions and thoroughly examining his uncle's body. Mom and Stevie might not have thought to examine James. The family's examination of James' neck immediately after he was pronounced dead, and the photographs taken by Michael, are blessings most families do not receive under these circumstances. To add to our blessings, every official document I have received from every individual initially involved with James' body corroborates the photographs. They all describe the only mark on James' entire body is an abrasion on his chin. They mention absolutely no marks on his neck, which makes these the most valuable pieces of evidence in this wrongful death claim. I mean, hey, if it doesn't fit, you must acquit, right?

Not necessarily! Because when you have every professional in a town working to protect their town and its jail staff by any means necessary, how can they lose? My brother has nothing to lose; he's dead. On the other hand, the Cumberland County jail staff had everything to lose if a wrongdoing was uncovered inside their jail.

So what was our family up against? It was obvious those working to protect the jail staff did not know James Dawson, because if they had, they would have known that James was totally against suicide. They would have known there was no way James would have arranged for his family to pick him up, only to find him dead. They would have known about the open communication James had with his family and friends. They would have known how much James valued life. And they would have known that one day, James' side of the story would be told, simply because the blood of Jesus has miraculous powers.

As God helps me navigate the retracing of my brother's death, I've had to ask, "Why have thou forsaken me to deliver this story? I am not an attorney, an investigating officer, or a coroner, nor do I consider myself an author. I am just James Dawson's sister, who knew my brother all his life." I was asked, "Who better to deliver the story of your brother's death?" I realized this calling was for me to transform my journey into something that would curtail false suicide labels placed on the deaths of loved ones while in police custody. I gave my word that I would give this documentary my best shot. I would try to set free the minds of all the alleged suicide hanging victims' families and bring awareness to this epidemic.

I am utilizing the first amendment, freedom of speech, in this documentary to address the issue of power. I am addressing the thought-police theory, which consists of "What I am telling you is the truth, and if you don't agree with me, then you are wrong." The thought-police try to control our thoughts and theories, but we have to see both sides because there is no singular truth. That is why it is imperative for me to lay out all the details of my brother's death. I applied the principals, and you have the privilege of applying the rest. All I ask is that you adapt to reality and see these allegations for what they really are—inconclusive and prejudiced. The most compelling argument is that anybody who really knew James Dawson knows he would have never taken his own life. So, yes, we present to you the facts. This case is only as strong as its evidence.

Meanwhile, back in Chicago, the news quickly spread about James' death. Once people began to hear the circumstances surrounding his death, they knew something was wrong. Their faith and belief in my family is the backbone of our strength. There were many telephone calls, telegrams, letters, cards, visitors, flowers, and donations sent to contribute to legal fees. To know James was to love him, and everybody wanted the best defense team in the business to bring forth justice.

On November 7, 2000, the day after James' death, at approximately noon, a call was received from the coroner's office. He told Mom that the official cause of death was suicide, hanging by the neck, and that there were no signs of foul play. That's it. That's all. Mom repeated to the family what the coroner said to her, so I told Mom to let me talk to him. I asked how they could have come to that conclusion when there were no marks on James' neck. The coroner told me he could not discuss the case in length, but that we would receive a copy of the autopsy report in four to six weeks. He concluded with "I'm sorry," told me preparations were being made for Leak's staff to pick up the body, and then abruptly ended our conversation. That was the second time the coroner had evaded my question about the lack of marks on James' neck.

Later that evening, on November 7, around five p.m., a call was received from Leak's staff, asking if we were sure James' body was at the Memorial Medical Center in Springfield because they were unsuccessful in locating it. They did not retrieve the body until the following day. Due to the late arrival and runaround tactics, I requested an independent autopsy. Leak's staff explained it would cost $975 to have a re-autopsy performed, which I paid for. The re-autopsy took place the following day, on November 9.

On November 9, the independent pathologist called, and I knew something was wrong. I watched Mom fall to her knees and drop the phone. I picked up the phone and spoke to the independent pathologist while the family consoled Mom. He told me what he had told her—that "strangulation," his exact word, was the cause of death. He said that when he re-opened James' body, there was nothing there. It was an empty cavity. The body contained no internal organs, no tissue, no brain, and no blood. The independent pathologist asked if James had been sick. I told him James only had common colds; other than that, he had always been healthy. He asked if Mom was okay then told me that further tests had to be done, and we would receive a copy of his report within thirty days.

Leak's job was only to prepare the body for the funeral; we would have never known James' body was completely cleaned out by the Springfield pathologist had I not requested an independent autopsy. The destruction of James' internal cavity was done without notification to my family and without any authorization. Is this what the coroner meant when he told Mom it was the law to have James' body transported to Springfield? Was it so they could get rid of the actual cause of death? The first rule of a cover-up is to get rid of incriminating evidence. What other reason could there have been for them to empty James' internal cavity?

Although the independent pathologist said further tests had to be done, what tests can be performed on an empty cavity? More importantly, since the family had already witnessed and photographed the absence of marks on James' neck, no questions about the condition of James' neck were posed to the independent pathologist on November 9. The mystery lay in the independent pathologist's conclusion that strangulation was the cause of death. How could strangulation be the cause of death when there were no marks? I realize that modern technology can easily prove what could not be demonstrated years ago.

On November 10, at ten p.m., Leak's staff notified us that James' body was ready for viewing; it was exactly twelve hours before the funeral was scheduled to take place. I was extremely sick and had been receiving chemotherapy for months, so the family was worried about me physically and mentally. On our way to the funeral home, I began having flashbacks of moments my brother and I had shared. I recalled him calling me two to three times a day to check on how I was feeling, encouraging me to never give up, no matter how sick I got. I had been recently carjacked and tried to fight off my attacker. The gun fell out of his hands. James was so angry with me because he felt I had jeopardized my life for a car. I tried to explain that the guy was as small as I was so when the gun fell, I thought I could take him. I later realized that was crazy. I recalled every time James and I had a conversation or anybody else had a conversation with James about how someone had taken his or her own life. He always got angry and said, "Ain't nothing that serious." He often said, "You don't have to ever worry about me going out like that." So him dying in such a manner is unimaginable.

We were at the funeral home now, and as I walked up to the casket, I was completely destroyed. The incision on my brother's head brought tears to my eyes. In a head autopsy, the incision is supposed to be made where it is not visible, even on a shaven head. The pillow from the casket is supposed to be able to cover the head incision, but the incision on James' head was too far forward to be hidden. Amazingly, Leak's staff was able to capture his beautiful smile. I could actually feel his presence and hear him saying, "Margaret, you will find the answers you are searching for because today is a good day."

I could not understand at first. How today could be a good day? He was dead. But every day is a good day, a day the Lord had made. It was not in his nature to make anything bad. When the Lord created the sun, the moon, the day, and the night, the Lord stood back, looked at his creation, and said, "This is good." We must start every day of our lives with a belief in the goodness of God, loving human beings, being glad to be alive, and being thankful for the work we have to do.

When I began searching for answers, I learned that finding answers was not the problem; finding those who would listen to me was. Every legal representative I was directed to listened to my story and felt my pain, and then their doors silently closed. I began to feel like I didn't have ability or intelligence. Then I began to wonder at the use of even getting out of the bed. This is an insult to our creator, implying he made us badly. God does not make us wrong; we make ourselves wrong. When God made us, he made us right. He did not make us weak. If we hamper ourselves and pamper ourselves with fears and timidity, we will make ourselves weak. We can sit back, look at the animals, and see that God gives the very least of his creatures amazing wells of strength, energy, and capability. So, as unimpressive a candidate we may think we are, God has his eyes on us.

At first, I could not understand, but now my heart is too full of understanding, because it is in my heart where my brother will live forever. We don't try to prove immortality because we want to believe it; we try proving it because we can't help believing it. So all the things I cannot and will never be able to understand leads to Proverb "Trust in the Lord with all your heart and lean not to your own understanding. In all your ways acknowledge him, and he shall direct your path." My path leads to my brother's spirit. I feel as though his last breath was placed inside me, and that is why I can deliver his story.

I cannot let his death be in vain. I cannot let others die unaware of the growing epidemic of suicide hangings while in police custody. I can live fighting a good fight, but I cannot live without fighting at all. I thank God for being all I needed. He gave me the strength, the courage, and the wisdom to outline every detail, from the jail to the Office of the Coroner. Every one of those avenues that the body of James Dawson was processed through suggests a cover-up attempt. Whether the cover-up was intentional or not, you be the judge. However, the cover up by the town's coroner and the pathologist in Springfield should be against the law. There is no doubt in my mind that they should be held accountable for getting rid of internal evidence that could have led to discovering James' actual cause of death. Since when did it become right to get rid of evidence? In what court of law can anyone get rid of evidence, leaving as proof only his or her words?

When I first learned how my brother died, I knew there was a story behind it, but I could have never imagined it would be anything like this. The Lord carries me through this journey. This battle is not mine; it is the Lord's. My brother's death is no greater or lesser than any other is. This story was written to bring to light all of the suspicious circumstances surrounding his death, and to the forefront the laws by which we are governed. If the suicide hangings in police custody continue to go unchallenged, who will be the next victim?

Death

Every day, death occurs. Just as sure as we are born, we must also die. Expected or unexpected, it is something we cannot change. Death is an unusual experience, and the impact it has varies for every individual. The feelings you have during a death are meant for you and you alone. No two people have the exact same feelings. Death brings a personal grieving, so depending on the attachments and bonding, grief has no limits. It is a natural response for people to say, "I know exactly how you feel." Take that phrase out of your mind, because even if you have experienced death, which we all have, you really have no idea.

Knowing you will never be able to see, touch, or tell someone "I love you" ever again is reality. This is real! Whether reality sets in or not, we must go on and continue to live in this world. At least when there is closure, our lives can go on with a little peace of mind. When our loved ones die and we wonder what really happened, when our loved ones have everything to live for and the next minute they are dead, when there is no closure, our minds are never really at peace, and our personal experience with death changes our lives. We live in a world that tries to prepare us for life, but it is almost impossible to prepare us for death. We may purchase life insurance policies and even plots for our burials, but nobody knows the exact date and time death will occur. Nobody knows but the Lord, because it has already been written in the book of Revelations. We cannot choose when, where, or how we are going to die, but we all must die, and no one can escape it.

We sometimes sit back and take life for granted; nobody wakes up and plans to die. We think we will grow old, and then die. Who thinks about death at an early age? Life is to live; this is the routine we follow. Those who have died would love to start their day over again and escape death. Love should not have to originate in death; love should be for the living. So love the people in your life as you have never loved them before, because once death occurs, you cannot start again. When a person dies, the body is dead and buried, but the spirit lives on forever. The body is just the shell that the spirit occupied while living.

.

Life

We are all born into this life innocent and without choice. In this world, when we reach the age of accountability, when life has taken away all its innocence, we are held accountable for the choices we make for our lives. It's all about choice. It has already been placed in our hearts and minds that we want the best for ourselves. Whether our goals turn from ourselves to our children to our parents, the best is all anybody ever wants.

Preparing for success is definitely a challenge. This world catches many people in the rapture of negative avenues. Just look around; the world is filled with hunger, drugs, and homeless people. People kill one another and wind up in prison. Many negative avenues have touched someone we know—and others we do not know. It is only by the grace of God that we are not a part of negative avenues. Even for those who are caught up, the Lord is in your reach and can hear your cry. As long as the blood runs warm through our veins, we still have a chance to find out about the greatness of the Lord. At some point in our lives, there will be an introduction to God. The roadmap to eternal life has different directions for each of us to travel. The Bible is our official roadmap, written by men of faith, not by men of science. The explanation of the miracle of creation through science does not contradict the Bible; it only makes us more aware of how great the miracle of creation was.

Our personal experiences and challenges are for us to learn from and to grow with. Our personal relationships with God are all that really matter, and we are not strangers to him because he already knows who we are. When the time comes for the Lord to read our rap sheets on Judgment Day, we will be held accountable for the choices we made. Preparation is needed for every transition because how we live life merits what happens next. There is no need to hold up the shield of being saved, sanctified, and filled with the Holy Ghost. Lower the shield a bit and help somebody as you pass. If we cheer somebody with a word or song, show somebody they are traveling wrong, then our life will not be in vain. There is no salvation without compassion for others, so unless we have made no mistakes, be careful of the stones we throw. We all have some vice, and it took something for us to find God.

There is a whole world out there, full of people who do not believe in God. There are those whom the Lord has chosen to teach and preach his words, and there are those that have chosen themselves. The Bible does not teach the exact same thing to everyone because there are so many different versions of the Bible's teachings. Anyone who has argued the meaning of the Bible knows how difficult it is to resolve disagreements. I often ask how it is that people of equal intelligence, sincerity, honesty, and faith do not reach the same understanding when it comes to the words of God. How can we describe, let alone understand, a being as complex as God Almighty? If so many capable Christians can read the same Bible and still arrive at different and conflicting conclusions, it is enough to create confusion. Our belief in God is freely chosen because we believe what we want to believe. Granted, it is not easy to step outside of our own understanding and adapt to another's. It requires imagination and a disciplined effort, especially when it runs contrary to your way of viewing things. If the Bible is the infallible, inerrant word of God, if it is the absolute truth for everyone, everywhere, universally, then why is there so much controversy among the billions of people who read and study it? The bottom line is that God is a spiritual being, and being created in his image means that we were created as spiritual beings with an eternal soul, able to open our hearts and minds to a better understanding of God, his complexity. His magnitude is phenomenal.

James's Funeral

On November 11, 2000, at ten a.m., the funeral took place at Grant Memorial African Methodist Episcopal Church, officiated over by Rev. Mickarl D. Thomas. The church was filled to capacity. People from all walks of life paid their final respects. Friends, co-workers, dignitaries, church members, and family members from several states were here. It was the most beautiful home-going celebration imaginable. One would have thought it was a celebrity's funeral. The family was completely overwhelmed to witness how many lives James had touched in his thirty-seven years. Mr. Morgan Propter, from the Rainbow Push Coalition, videotaped the funeral.

When the family members began to speak, I sat in amazement, watching so many people joining in the celebration of James' life. I had written the obituary program, so I wanted to give others the opportunity to speak, but a strong force from behind the scenes stepped in, and I got permission from the pastor to interrupt the scheduled program. I can't tell you what I said; the words just started coming out of my mouth. After the funeral, many people came up and told me that my words had touched them deeply. I was elated to have been able to do so. Days after the funeral, letters about James really started to pour in. Hundreds of letters filled Mom's dining table. The letters are still coming, years after my brother's death. I thank God that I have been able to respond to every letter received, except for those with no return address. Here are some of the letters. Unfortunately, I could not submit all of them, but they are all just as special:

The Letters

We all loved James so much. My mother lives in the building where he worked. We have three children who adored him. Our oldest is six years old, was raised in James arms, and dearly misses him. I hope you are doing well. What a terrible loss! I hope you have the person or people who have done this. Please let us know if we can do anything. Your son was always smiling, sweet, and helpful. You should be proud of the impression he left in our lives.

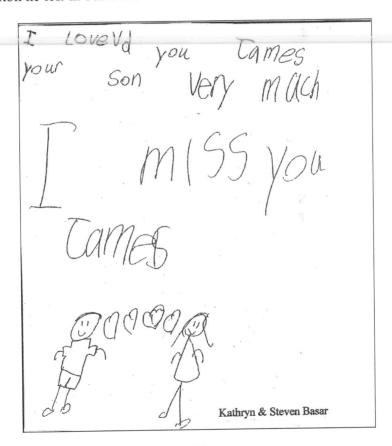

I loveVd you James
your Son very much

I miss you

I James

Kathryn & Steven Basar

Dear Mrs. Dawson:

I am a resident of Sandburg Village, and I knew your son James. I am still grieved by his wrongful death. Please accept my humble condolences. May the Lord avenge his death and bring judgment to the guilty ones. We will miss him very much. Thank you for being such a wonderful mother. Please accept this small gift to help pay for your legal fight.

We've got some difficult days ahead. But it really doesn't matter with me now, because I've been to the mountaintop, and I've seen the Promised Land. I may not get there with you, but I want you to know that we as a people will get to the Promised Land.
Rev. Martin Luther King, Jr.

The Kim Family

To the Dawson Family:

You are in our thoughts and prayers. James was and is very dear to us. He was an extraordinary man filled with kindness and warmth. We treasure his smile and the bounce in his steps. Please tell James Jr. the Jalds know how much his dad loved him. We grieve with you.

To the Dawson Family:

James and I have known one another all our lives and we are best friends. On the night of November 5, I called James around 10:45 p.m. to see if he still wanted me to go to court with him. He told me he was on his way out of town and had completely forgotten about the court date. I told him he should be glad that I called him. We laughed and joked about it, and James thanked me because he hadn't gotten too far, so he was going to turn around and go back home. The next day I kept calling James' cell phone, and I could not understand why he didn't answer because he wanted me to go to court with him. That is why I kept calling Momma Dawson's house. When Margaret told me that James was dead, I just assumed he was in a car accident or something, but nothing like this.

When James and I were together in the later part of September, he was stopped for speeding on the expressway. You know James always says he's moving with the flow of traffic. When the officer stopped him, he told James his license was suspended for no proof of insurance, an SR-22 responsibility suspension. James showed the officer that he indeed had insurance, so the officer told him he still had to give him a ticket. He told him that he could drive on the ticket but he must report to court on November 6 to straighten out why his license had an SR-22 suspension. I cannot understand why James was taken to jail for the exact same thing he was scheduled to

25

straighten out the very next day. He had one more day to drive on that ticket.

I need you all to forward this letter to Margaret because when I told her about the incident, she wanted me to write a statement so she could give it to the attorney. All of James' insurance information should be in the glove compartment in his car.

Richard

To the Family of James Dawson:

I talked to James on the night he was stopped by the police. He was to meet up with me and the guys in Tunica. He called me about eleven p.m. to let me know that he had driven almost three hours and had forgotten about a court date for the following day. He told me he could not miss the court date because he had to get his license back. He went into further detail about what happened when he was issued the ticket, and we laughed about it. He told me he was just going to fill up and head back home. When I heard that the police stopped James less than a half hour after I had talked to him, I just could not believe it. James would have never taken his own life. For what? I hope the people who killed my best friend are caught. So many times, I wish I could turn back the hands of time because I know if James had not been taken to that jail, he would be alive today. I love you all, and may God comfort and bless you.

Ray

To the Dawson Family:

It is hard for me to write this letter to you today because I know there is no way James would have taken his own life. Many times, James and I have talked about suicide because I wanted to take my own life. When my daughter's father died in a car accident on his way to the hospital when I was in labor, it was the most difficult time of my life. James was there for me, and he made me realize that it was not about me, but about my child. He constantly stayed on me and made sure I was okay.

Shanna is James' goddaughter, and we miss him so, so much. It comforts me to know that now James and Shanna's dad have so much to talk about. Shanna and I will forever keep James alive in our hearts. I hope I can visit so you all can get to know Shanna. Thanks for letting me share this with you.

Cookie & Shanna

Dear Mrs. Dawson

My name is Dominique Martin. I knew James from Sandburg Village. He was a great guy, always smiling and with something nice to say. I am so very sorry for your loss and based upon what I've been told, I am outraged by what happened to him. I would like to try to help.

In an attempt to learn and confirm the facts, without further disturbing you, I have left messages requesting someone from Operation Push's Field Office to contact me. However, since I haven't heard back from them, I wanted to at least give you the following information.

I am told that basically should you wish the appropriate authorities should be held responsible. Generally once a person is in a jailer's custody, the jailer is responsible and has the duty to make sure there is nothing a person can do to harm themselves or anyone else. The preferable action is a federal rather than state lawsuit. One or more organizations listed below should be able to help should you wish to pursue further.

ACLU
NAACP
Lawyer's Committee for Civil Rights
Southern Poverty Law Center
United States Attorney's Office

If you decide to pursue the matter you may also want to contact as many people and organizations as possible for investigation into the facts, support and publicity. Examples include your state and federal senators and representatives, the press including news columnists, television and radio talk show hosts and personalities etc.

Mrs. Dawson:

Please accept my condolences regarding the passing of James. I have lived at Sandburg for twenty years, and have therefore known James since he has been there. I will miss his smile and laugh, which brightened my day. I am a professor of toxicology at the University of Illinois Medical School, toxicology being the science of poisons. I heard the second autopsy indicates poisoning. If you are seeking legal action, please pass my resume along to your lawyer. I provide consultation services for lawyers in the area of toxicology.

Sincerely,

Dr. Barry Levine

Dear Mrs. Dawson:

I feel honored to have known James and to have been able to attend his funeral. I had hoped to lend support and comfort to those close to James, but I ended up being the recipient of comfort. Thank you for raising such wonderful and faithful children. Their words of faith, and your faith, was truly inspiring.

Yours in Christ
Jean Mahony

Dearest Family and Friends of James:

Words cannot express how sad I was when I heard James had passed away. I did not know him very well; however, I always saw his smiling face whenever I went down to the garage to get a package. He must have been an amazing person because he always had a smile on his face and was friendly to everyone. I always left him thinking I should try to smile more like that. Please know that you are in my thoughts and prayers.

Cindy Schlesinger

To the Family of James Dawson:

I am a resident at the Carl Sandburg Village where James worked. I have learned of his passing, and I am very sorry to hear this news. I found James to be a very nice person and pleasant to talk to. I am writing this note to you today to offer my condolences in your time of need. I would also like to share with you how I knew James. I am including three of my favorite memories, some I have shared with my family and friends in the past. I hope sharing these few memories with you will, in some small way, bring comfort, knowing how James touched so many lives.

Last Christmas, my nephews were in town visiting; their ages are six and seven. On Christmas Eve, James, myself, and my nephews all exchanged holiday greetings. James laughed and smiled at the boys' excitement for Christmas. The next morning, we ran into one another again, and this time my nephews had their brand new Star Wars ships in their hands as we exchanged good mornings. Along with the hello, James said to my nephews in a very pleasant and cheery tone, "So did you break them yet?" One of my nephews replied, equally cheerfully, "Oh, yeah," and proceeded to explain how he had broke his ship. At this, James laughed with his baritone "Ha, ha." His laugh was infections. We all laughed, though my nephews didn't understand the humor of breaking the ship, they were just happy to be laughing with James.

I began seeing James more regularly this year because I began driving, and I needed to park my car in the garage where he worked every night. I didn't have a permanent stall so I had to leave my car for James to handle. Since my car was always parked in a different spot every night, it was a bit of a hunt for me to find it. I thought I could find it if I triggered the horn button on my key chain. One morning, about six a.m., I decided to test the horn button and because we were in the garage, the sound echoed quite loudly. I was startled and couldn't figure out how to turn it off. I was embarrassed at the commotion I was causing in the garage. James caught me in my silliness and just laughed. I told James I thought I had learned something new about my car that morning although I wished I didn't have to learn it at six a.m. and in such a loud way. I apologized to James for making such a ruckus. He said, "Oh that's okay," as he laughed because he already knew what was going on.

One night, when I pulled into the garage, I told James I often thought of the *Lucy Show* when I got home. I often felt like announcing to him and the other parking attendants, "Honey, I'm home," like Ricky announced to Lucy in the show. I had no roommate to say this to, and it just felt right to greet the guys this way. James laughed, and he told me that he didn't think the guys would mind if I greeted them this way. Of course, I didn't take up the practice, but we enjoyed a good laugh. I will miss James. I can imagine he will be a great loss to your family. My thoughts and prayers are with you today and every day.

Catherine

Dear Mrs. Dawson

We send our sincerest condolences to you. We were shocked and saddened to hear about James. He always had a big smile and a friendly hello to offer. He often made our days much brighter with his beautiful smile. We will truly miss him. We hope you will find comfort in your many memories. This is such a tragic and senseless loss, and it's so difficult to understand. Your family is in our thoughts and prayers.

Peggy and Fred Schubryd

Dear Mrs. Dawson:

My husband and I were preparing to leave Sandburg Village for our new home and my new position at Barry University in Florida. We did not want to leave without telling you that James and your lovely family will continue to be in our daily prayers. As a mother, you know better than anyone of us what a wonderful, kind, generous, and thoroughly good person James was. On a number of occasions, he lifted our spirits and made us smile. My fondest memories were the days James Jr. came to work with his dad. On many occasions, James addressed me with

"Hi, Ma," and it was a warm honor. Please know that James is remembered with love and respect, as is the Dawson Family.

Carrol Jald

Dear Mrs. Dawson:

I just returned from San Diego and was informed that your son James lost his life while being held in police custody. I don't know many of the details relating to this tragedy, but what I do know is that James would never have taken his own life. I have known James for many years and his death definitely deserves an investigation so I am willing to do whatever it takes to help. James was always cheerful and really brightened my day whenever I saw him. He always had a smile on his face and a distinctive laugh. I am so sorry for the loss of such a great human being. Please call me.

Jack Davis

Dear Mrs. Dawson

I cannot begin to express how deeply saddened I am about the death of my friend James. I will truly miss his wonderful smile, which was always present, and his kind words. When I moved from Cummings House in May, I immediately felt a loss not seeing and chatting with James daily. Now I feel an even greater loss as I am sure everyone who knew James does. I was coming back to Cummings House to visit with James when I got the news of his passing. I now give to you, his family, this gift. May it comfort you to know that James touched so many lives.

Lynn Evangelista Quinn

Dear Mrs. Dawson:

We live in one of the buildings where your son James worked, and we are shocked to hear of his death. James was absolutely wonderful. He always had a big smile, knew our names, and really brightened the place. We know your loss is enormous, and we are praying for you. Your son was terrific and an obvious tribute to you. We are so sorry for your loss.

Sally Hewitt, Larry Jakus

Dear Mrs. Dawson:

I want to express my sincere sympathy in the loss of your son James. I have known him ever since he started working at Sandburg. Until recently, I was a resident, and James and I became friends. We laughed and joked every time we saw one another. His kindness extended to my family and friends that visited and parked in the garage. His upbeat personality, large smile, and easy laugh are what I will always remember. He will truly be missed. Please know that others will often think of James, and he will be kept in our prayers.

Melinda Swapys

To the Dawson Family:

It broke my heart when I heard that James had passed. I knew him for many years and considered him part of my Sandburg family. His smile was beautiful, and he had a great sense of humor. He greeted me when I left and he greeted me when I came home. I knew when he had a cold because he wore his hat. I will truly miss his teasing. Several members of my family even got a chance to know James. He truly brightened my days, and I will miss him very much. I am not good at attending funerals, but I want to do something for your family. The circumstances surrounding James' death do not sit right with me. Enclosed is a gift in memory of James, my friend, my buddy. I extend my sincere sympathy to your family.

Dee Davis

Dear Mrs. Dawson:

There is a joyous celebration in our father's house today as one so dearly loved is welcomed home. I remember when I was young and James would walk across the alley to see Faye. Before he could make it halfway across, I would unlock the door so when he got there he could just walk right on in. Take comfort in knowing the Lord had the door open the same way I used to, so that James could just walk right on in. Mourning is for those who must go on without the ones we love. Though James has left this life, he has claimed eternal rest and peace, rejoicing in the arms of our savior. I am praying that you will find comfort at this most difficult time.

Cassidy Mac

Dear Mrs. Dawson:

I am writing to express my condolences regarding your son James. I lived in Sandburg for two years. When I first moved to Chicago four years ago, I was going through a divorce. Your son's smile and kindness helped me to see the goodness in life. James was a good and kind soul, filled with compassion for others. His warmth and ability to lift a person's spirit, just by breaking into that contagious laugh, were the gifts he possessed. This is what I will always remember and treasure. I am so sorry for your loss, and I know it is shared by many. May God be with you.

Bonnie Butler

To the Family of James Dawson:

I have parked my car in the garage for years. James was always kind, helpful, and extremely competent in his job. I cannot tell you how saddened I felt when I heard of his tragic death. What a terrible loss to all of us. My deepest sympathy goes out to all family members and friends. Mrs. Jo Greller would also like to extend her sympathy to all of you in the death of James. Mrs. Greller is ninety years old, and she fondly recalls all the very special ways of James. She keeps repeating, "He was so nice, such a good man." I think that says it all.

Joel Crome & Jo Greller

To the Dawson family:

When James and I were together on the night of November 3, he was in great spirits, as usual. He was so excited about his son coming home for Thanksgiving. That was going to be his vacation week, so they would be able to spend the entire week together. It is so hard for me to believe that James is no longer here. Anybody who knew James knows he would have never taken his own life. He was strong in his views about that kind of thing. When I heard how he died, I immediately knew it was a lie. I pray the people responsible for my friend's death are caught. I know that bad things can happen to good people. I will keep James alive with every breath I take. I hope you all find comfort in knowing James will be kept alive in many hearts. I wanted to also let you all know that James paid for a trip we had planned for New Years in Las Vegas. There is still time for me to sell his spot so that his money will not be lost. I will be contacting you all later to give you this money.

Sam

Mr. & Mrs. Sidney Dawson and Family

Dear Mr. & Mrs. Dawson,

Charlotte and I apologize for being so late in writing to you to thank you for your Christmas card and the lovely remembrance card for James.

We, like so many others at Sandburg Village, were shocked and deeply saddened when we heard of James' passing. James was a wonderful man and his smile brought sunshine into our lives even on the darkest days. We are sure you will always be comforted by your memory of him just as we will.

When we were in church we were especially impressed with the eulogies given by your children. You obviously have raised a wonderful God-loving family of which you should be very proud.

We hope you will find peace in the knowledge that James has truly gone on to a better place prepared for him by our Lord. God bless you all.

With love,

John Roger Brandenburg

Dear Mrs. Dawson:

We live in one of the condo buildings where James worked, and we had the good fortune of knowing him. We were unable to attend his funeral, but my husband and I wanted to let you and your family know that we will miss James and his great laugh and smile. We want to share a story about James. My husband started parking his car in the garage about a year ago and he mentioned a really nice guy named James. He said James knew his name and said, "Hi, Adam." It made my husband happy that James remembered his name because James met many people each day. I met James when I went to the parking garage with Adam. Our car is parked about eight cars from James' office so I would stand in front of his office until Adam came with the car. After a couple of times, James said, "Hi, Christine" when he saw me, and we would talk about sport games he was interested in and the weather, but mostly where Adam and I were going. The funny story is that James noticed I never drove our car, then one day, Adam was gone, and I needed to pick a friend up from the train station. My husband gave me strict instructions to ask James to take the car out of the parking space. Our parking space is next to a pole and it's sort of tricky to park there. I said to James, "The time has come. I'm taking her out (meaning the car), and James laughed because he knew I hadn't driven the car, and we'd had it for over a year. I told James Adam gave me strict instructions to let him drive the car out of the parking space because he thought I would total it before I even got out of the garage. As James pulled the car out and I got in, I told James it might take me a while to figure out all of the controls. I was figuring out how to move the steering wheel and adjust the seat, and I could see James just laughing and smiling. I told him if I didn't return within an hour to please call our insurance company, but luckily, I returned safely with the car intact. James knew once I had returned I was going to ask him to park the car, and ever since then, James would ask me when I was taking it out a second time. It was about my driving that we joked a lot.

I talked to James a few days before his passing, and just like everyday, he was smiling and laughing. This is what we will miss about James now that he is no longer with us. We will miss the happiness he shared with Adam and me. We discovered that it takes a special person like James to make people happy. If we have learned anything, it's that a few moments with someone who makes us smile and laugh can last forever in our hearts, and James is certainly in our hearts and memories. We will keep you in our prayers.

Christine & Adam

At the age of nine, my nephew wrote a short story entitled "No Easy Answers," dedicating it to his Uncle Pookie and his grandparents. The story consists of pictures cut out of construction paper asking "Why?" My nephew's story and other stories from students at the Madison School in Las Vegas were published in a book entitled *Let the Dew drops Fall*. The teacher's name was Romona Rollins Muhammad. First Lady Laura Bush acknowledged the book:

THE WHITE HOUSE

January 14, 2002

Ms. Romona Rollins Muhammad, Teacher
and Students
Madison School
1040 North J Street
Las Vegas, Nevada 89106-2832

Dear Ms. Muhammad and Students:

Thank you for sending me the newspaper article about your
recently published book, *Let the Dew Drops Fall.* Working
together to write stories and create the artwork for your
collection is quite an accomplishment! I am happy that copies
of your book will be available at your local library for other
classmates to read.

Reading helps prepare you for every grade in school. The more
you read, the better you will do on your tests (especially
vocabulary and spelling tests). Reading and writing skills will
help you in college and in any career you choose.

Remember to thank the teachers, librarians, and everyone who
helps to make your school a place where you love to be and love
to learn. And keep up the good work!

With best wishes,

Laura Bush

Two years later, he continued to receive recognition.

THE BOOK CORNER

Dr. Colleen Birchett

GOD'S WONDERFUL CHILDREN

Osayande Williams is 11 years old. Everyone calls him Osay, for short. He won first place in the Young Author's Contest at his school. Then he went to the regional contest and won. Then he went all the way to Illinois State University in Normal, Illinois.

Osayande Williams

He met many other young authors. This is the second time that he has made it that far in the contest! Osay created the pictures for his own book. He cut them out of construction paper.

The people at Border's Bookstore liked his book very much. They asked him to read at their bookstore. Many, many people came to hear Osay read his book. Then the people at 57th Street Book Fair heard about it. They asked him to read his book at their book fair. At the fair, he read his book to people from all over the city.

His book is called *No Easy Answers*. It is about his uncle whom he calls "Uncle Pookie." His uncle was killed. No one knows exactly how his uncle died. The police had arrested the uncle because they said he was driving without a license. But it was strange how his uncle died before anyone could find out the real truth. He died while he was with the police, but no one knows how he died.

Osay was very sad. He would miss his uncle. He wrote a book about his uncle.

Osay goes to McDade Classical School. He is in the 4th grade. Osay is a good student. He scored at the 7.9 grade level in Mathematics and Reading on the ITBS Test. He belongs to the McDade track team. He is on the basketball team. He also sings in the McDade choir. He has won many Science Fair competitions.

He is also active in a tennis program. His favorite hobby is to search on the Internet for secret codes. He puts them into his video games. He has been at Trinity United Church of Christ for all of his life. He is a member of Isuthu. In Isuthu he has moved from the Fante Nation to the Ga Nation. He belongs to Little Warriors, Athletes for Christ and Church School.

Biography

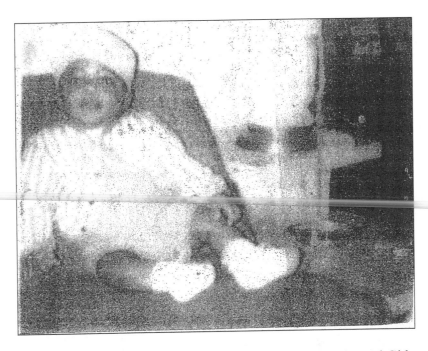

James Dawson was born on July 29, 1963, to Lillie and Sidney Dawson. He was the third of five children. "Pookie" was his nickname. James was raised on the south side of Chicago, where he graduated from Florence B. Price Elementary School and Martin Luther King High School. He furthered his education at George Williams College then entered the United States Navy. While serving in the navy, James married his longtime high school sweetheart, and to this union came a son, James Dawson, Jr. The couple moved to Oakland, California, where James completed his naval enlistment after four years. The couple later divorced, and James moved back to Chicago. James and Areda remained the best of friends, and James Jr. spent every summer vacation with his dad. They were inseparable.

When James moved back to Chicago, he held numerous jobs and later remarried. He worked at the Carl Sandburg Village for thirteen years, until his death. James enjoyed sports, and baseball was his passion. He enjoyed music and played DJ on numerous occasions. However, his favorite enjoyment was spending quality time with his family. He often took his nephews to Dave and Buster's. Every holiday, we had family gatherings at my parents' home, and we could always depend on James being the laughter of those gatherings. He enjoyed making others laugh and seeing everybody happy.

The Family Foundation

Growing up in the Dawson household was amazing, to say the least. Once we had all reached school age, Mom escorted us to school everyday. As soon as that bell rang at three, she was right there to pick us up. If she was not able to escort us, a familiar face took her place. The witness protection program had nothing on Mom. She had always been overprotective of her children, and she did not stop escorting us to and from school until we entered high school. She probably would have continued, but we convinced her that we would be okay now. When we did get a chance to go play with the other kids, Mom was not far behind, watching over us so we did not get a chance to get into too much trouble. Even when we went to the grocery store, Mom and Dad gathered all of us up and put us in the car. The other kids teased us about our parents, but we didn't mind because we knew it was nothing but love for their children. Most of our spare time was spent studying. Mom instilled in us that knowledge was the key to life, and once we had obtained that, nobody could take it away. When it came time for my son Michael, their first grandchild, to go to school, he went through some of the teachers we had gone through. Often he came home upset because the teachers said, "You can't be a Dawson. They would never get grades like this." The pedestals the teachers had placed us on were awfully high for Michael, but later he appreciated the pressure.

Dad was the real deal! When each of us reached the beautiful age of thirteen, Dad took us to get work permits, and off to work at the Dan Howard Manufacturing Company we went with him every summer. We never had a summer break. When school was out and summer break was in, every morning at four a.m., except for Sundays, we got up for work. The killing part about it was that we didn't start work until seven and the job wasn't but fifteen minutes away. Dad wanted us out of the house by five so he could get a free parking space. This had been his normal routine for the past thirty years, and it was not about to change just because we were going to work with him. Once we got to work, we walked to Lu Mitchell's restaurant to eat breakfast and hang out with Dad until it was time to hit the clock. We got off work at five every day, except for Saturdays. On Saturdays, we got off at noon. After work on Saturdays, we picked Mom up and went to visit her parents. I still visit my grandparents every Saturday. Dad's parents lived in Mississippi. Whenever we visited or talked to them, we could always depend on an introduction to the Lord. I don't care how many times we encountered them; our ears would overflow with the beauty of the powers of the Lord. May they both rest in peace.

While working those summer breaks, we never saw any of our money. We got paid every week, on Wednesdays. Dad had everything already mapped out for us. He opened each of us a savings account, and every week, our checks went into our account. We had direct deposit before there was a direct deposit. We watched our money grow every week, but we couldn't touch it until we graduated high school. Once we graduated, we were well on our way. Our friends and family started asking Dad if he could get them a job, and he was able to help several seek employment.

Every day at six p.m., it was dinnertime in the Dawson household. We sat around the table as if we were having a family reunion. Mom always told us that we could talk to her about anything. Dad, on the other hand, when it came to something he did not want to talk about, said, "Talk to your momma about that." All of our friends admired our family structure. All of our friends became family. Mom claimed everybody as her child, and Dad would say, "I'm glad all of them are her children."

Once we all reached adulthood and left home, our friends kept in touch with our parents, even without us being there. Of course, no family is picture-perfect, but the ammunition of love and togetherness is something we never ran out of.

Sidney Jr., the second born, has served in the United States Navy for twenty-two years. He was recently promoted to master-chief. He travels all over the world, teaching and training new naval recruits. Sharon, the fourth born, graduated in the top percent of her class in medical school. She was recently ordained a minister. Stevie, the baby, has never left Dad's side; they both still work together. And then there is myself, the composer of this documentary. So Mom and Dad, thanks for a job well done.

The Journey

As everyone travels with me through this valley of death, I have my moments. I have asked, "Who is James Dawson to the legal system?" Nobody. Who was James Dawson to those who did not know him? Nobody. But James Dawson was Somebody. He was not a famous athlete, celebrity, or anyone whose life and death deserves worldwide attention. He was just your average human being, living his life as well as possible, until it was all taken away in the wink of an eye. James started out as somebody's son, grandson, brother, nephew, and cousin, and moved on to be a husband, father, uncle, and friend. We are now introduced to his death, remembering that the life he lived can never be taken away. As we observe the headstone that reads "James Dawson July 29, 1963 – Nov 6, 2000," we see that the dates are the beginning and the end. What really matters is the dash between the two dates. That dash represents the thirty-seven years of my brother's life. That dash is how he lived and how he loved. One never knows how much time is left. Slow down; consider what is true and what is real. Try to understand how others feel. Be less quick to anger and show appreciation more. Treat each other with a little more respect and wear a smile more often, remembering that dash might only last for a little while. When our eulogy is being read and our life's actions rehashed, will we be proud of the things said about how we lived our dash? My brother gave no one a last farewell, nor did he know his last "goodbye" to Mom would be his last. James was gone before we knew it, and only God knows why. It broke our hearts to lose him, but he did not go alone. Part of us went with him when God called James home. I would like to share this poem, by an unknown author, with those who knew my brother and those who will get to know him through my eyes:

Do not stand at my grave and weep
For I am not there; I do not sleep.

I am the thousand winds that blow;
I am the diamond glints on snow,

I am the sunlight on ripened grain;
I am the autumn's rain.

When you've awakened in the morning's hush,
I am that swift, uplifting rush

The quiet birds in a circle flight;
I am the star that shines at night.

Think of me the same, I say,
For I am not dead, I am just away.

Tributes

S ince James was unable to say goodbye to his family, here is what I think he would say to them:

To my mother:

You are more than just my mother—you are my best friend. You raised me from a baby to a man. Our relationship was strong and powerful and so it will forever remain because we are as one. As you laid your eyes upon me when I took my first breath, you had the privilege of laying your eyes on me when I took my last breath. I heard your cry as you watched me taken away in the ambulance, and I felt your heartbeat because it was the heartbeat of my soul. My smile was your smile. The laughter I contagiously spread was your laughter, because you gave me my life. I love you, Mom. Remember, God makes no mistakes. That is why he appointed you my mother. God had a special job with my name on it. It's as you have always said—"God needs people he can depend on." It takes a special woman to do what you do, be who you are, to love like you do, and it all comes so natural because you are just being you.

To my father:

Pops, you have always been a quiet soul, but in your role as father, you have never been silent. You instilled in all of us at an early age that life is what you make of it. We did not understand at first why you made us work so hard. Now we realize that, by showing us the meaning of life instead of telling us about it, you did what the world is missing today. You taught us that when the doors of opportunity opened, we could just walk right in. The backbone we have to be hard, dependable workers comes from you. You had your own way of doing things, which most do not understand, but as life went on, your teachings made us what we are today. It is hard to find a man that is a dad, father, leader, provider, friend, and someone who remains in his children's lives and forever keeps his house their home. Although the world continued to change, your way of teaching should never change. You are now a grandfather. The same backbone you instilled in us needs to be instilled in our children because they are our future.

47

To my sisters: *Margaret & Sharon*
To my brothers: *Sidney & Stevie*

We have shared many precious moments together, and we have always respected one another. We seem to always catch that terrible disease of striving for the best and never settling for anything less. People have always admired our togetherness as a family. We left such an impact on our friends that our friends became family. Dad never understood why Mom had so many children, but we knew why—all the delicious meals she prepared daily, which smelled up the neighborhood, and all the quality time she made for us and our friends made her the neighborhood mom. The foundation we were raised on now needs to be passed to our children. Thanks for thirty-seven years worth of precious memories. When you think of me and start to feel sad, put those smiles back on your faces because where there is darkness, God will show you light to let you know that your brother James is all right. My fight was strong because I knew I was not alone. Yes, I feel your pain, but remember you have a lot to gain. I am in the house of the Lord; that is my greatest reward. This is not the end. I will see you all again.

To my son, James Dawson, Jr.

From the day you were born, you were my gift from God, a gift for a mom and dad. When I look at you, I see myself, and that is a gift meant for no one else. God gave you to me, and me to you, and no one will ever be able to sever that bond. I will be with you always. I am watching you always. You are my spirit and my soul; your heart pumps my blood. Remember me for the man I was, remember the life I lived, and remember that the path of righteousness lies in your hands. You may never know what is on the other side of the rainbow, and you never know where your journey is going to end. While there is an ending in this life, God gave me a beginning in a new life. We will always be that dynamic father and son duo because you now carry me in your heart. Hold your mother close. Right now, you may not be able to see, but J.J., God has rescued me. Right now, you may not be able to understand, but my life and death were already planned. Now I am in the clouds of joy, and I can still see my baby boy. As time goes on, all I ask is that you keep the faith and believe in God and yourself. You are the original part of me, and soon you will be able to see that if you should fall, get up and stand tall. When one door closes, another will surely open because you already have the master key, and that is being a part of me.

As James Jr. continues to hold that master key, here are some of his many accomplishments:

Pirates Poised

SAN LEANDRO FACES NO. 1 RANKED
DE LA SALLE 12

Athlete of the Week

Pirate offensive linemen James Dawson Jr., Donato Molina, Willie Roberts Jr. and Ray Turner.

San Leandro High's offensive line unit is this week's selection. The O line is anchored by two year starter Donato Molina; guards Willie Roberts Jr. and Lance Butler (not pictured) and tackles James Dawson Jr. and Ray Turner. This very talented and quick group once again led the HAAL in total team offense averaging 426 yards and 43 points per game. These "men in the trenches" make the long runs of SL's running backs possible, as well as providing excellent pass protection. The "O" line has been superb in the playoffs as well as SL has scored 96 points in 2 games so far. Senior Molina and Butler (also a two-year starter) and Turner will attend college next year. Offers should be forthcoming. Roberts, a sophomore and Dawson a junior, will return to the Pirates next season. We wish the best to all of these student athletes.

In his junior year at San Leandro High, Dawson didn't get much attention BUT IN HIS SENIOR YEAR:

James Dawson is a powerhouse on the football field. He usually lines up on the outside of the defensive line, although he also plays 0 – line sometimes. One can sometimes see him throwing off blockers and cutting the QB. He's a big-play player who can be counted on to get the job done when it's all on the line. Repeatedly, he has come up with a big sack when the team needed it most. He averages one sack and five tackles per game.

James carries a 3.0 GPA and is seeking to "make my life a challenge." He was born and raised in Chicago, Il., and is making the best of his opportunities at San Leandro High as an active member of A.S.U. and a player on the champion Pirate football team.

Athlete of the Week

San Leandro High basketball player **James Dawson** seldom scores the most points. The scrappy forward usually passes and lets somebody else do the shooting.

But last Friday against Tennyson, Dawson shot a game-high 21 points and led the Pirates to a 63-48 win to keep their playoff hopes alive.

The senior made it sound like there was nothing to it.

"Most of the shots were on offensive rebounds, so I just put the ball back up," Dawson said. "Everything was going right for me."

Dawson is headed to Utah State University next year on a football scholarship. He isn't the biggest defensive end, but his quickness and tenacity make him a top player.

His easy-going attitude puts people at ease. But once the ball is in play, he's all business.

James Dawson

"He just battles," said Pirate coach Todd Petersen. "That's what he's done all season."

Dawson likes his English classes and photography.

"I love photography. I'm a picture fanatic," he said.

Maybe that's what makes Dawson a good athlete. He loves just about everything he does.

SAN LEANDRO:

The greatest praise of the afternoon was saved for San Leandro defensive end James Dawson, who will room with Pennyman at Utah State next season. At just 6-0, 225 pounds, Dawson didn't get a ton of attention early, but his 15 sacks and amazing first step brought a lot of last-minute attention.

Illinois and UNLV were among the numerous schools that came in during the final days trying to land the undersized defensive end, but Dawson decided to stay loyal to the team that wanted him from Day 1.

"When we saw his first step, it was one of the best I have seen," another college scout commented. "His effort (sets him apart)," McPherson added. "James gives 120 percent all the time. The guy has speed, strength and he is awesome."

San Leandro Times

SPORTS

***

The Pirates took away the Rebel's next drive when James Dawson picked up a fumble and rumbled 75 yards for San Leandro's second touchdown!

***

San Leandro's defensive lineman James Dawson had the lineman's dream performance coming up with two key sacks and returning an Arroyo fumble 50-yards for a touchdown.

After the Dons (2-1 overall, 11 in league) forced San leandro (3-0, 2-0) to punt on its opening possession, the Dons proceeded to to march down to the Pirates 20-yardline. On third and eight, Arroyo quarterback Logan Irons dropped back to pass. But Dawson busted through the line and dropped him for a 8-yard loss!

***

Pirates defensive lineman James Dawson gave the Spartans as much to handle as a defender possibly could. Dawson caught De La Salle's fast quarterback Britt Cecil by the ankle behind the line for a sack to stop a Spartan drive in the first quarter. Dawson blocked a Spartan extra-point attempt in the second quarter and the defender made tackles throughout the game!

***

San Leandro Holds Off Pittsburg, 36-28, in a Close One:
"They gave us a run for our money," said San Leandro lineman James Dawson. "I couldn't get a pass rush on them. They doubled me." Double teamed or not, it's saying something when a team keeps Dawson out of the quarterback's face!

$566,358.00

Is the total value of all four awarded to: Dennis Dixon, Sam Cheatham, Reggie McPherson and James Dawson.

James Dawson- All HAAL, All ANG Selection, 15 Sacks last season and possibly the best pure pass rusher in school history.
College Choice- Utah State (Big Sky)

Congratulations to these young men and their families and congratulations to the entire Pirate Family!

Nine grads who overcame obstacles

TUESDAY
June 17, 2003

SAN LEANDRO High School graduates pose for a photo that was sent out on the invitations for their collective graduation party. They are Michael Thomasson (back row, left), Kerry Wooldridge, Dennis Dixon Jr., Reginald McPherson Jr., James Dawson Jr. (lower left), Lamonte Toney, Raymond Ellis Stokes, Samuel Cheatham and Raymar Crosby.

■ 'They are the exception to the rule' about young African-American men

By Jason Bono
STAFF WRITER

SAN LEANDRO — The parents of nine African-American San Leandro High graduates recently got together to throw their sons a party.

More than a graduation bash, it turned into a celebration of family, community and obstacles overcome.

"I think they are the exception to the rule," parent Kandice Toney said of her son Lamonte and his friends Samuel Cheatham, Raymar Crosby, Dennis Lee Dixon Jr., James Dawson Jr., Reginald McPherson Jr., Raymond Ellis Stokes, Michael Thomasson and Kerry Wooldridge.

The teenagers have grown up as competitors, teammates and friends since elementary and middle school. And they have succeeded despite stereotypes and statistics, Toney said.

CLASS OF 2003

And the statistics are formidable.

More than a third of African-American students in the San Leandro school district — and 18.9 percent of African-American students statewide — will drop out during a four-year period, according to state data from the 2001-02 school year.

Many say the numbers are unreliable and lower than in reality because school districts report their own data. But the numbers show African-American students, males in particular, dropping out at a higher rate than any other ethnic group statewide.

Of the students who do graduate, a smaller percentage of males than females meet the requirements to attend University of California or California State University campuses.

But those aren't the only odds the graduates have struggled against.

"A lot of people say children without a father tend not to do well," said McPherson. "All my life, I've been

striving to prove that wrong."

Saturday, more than 150 family members and friends joined McPherson and his friends in the Veteran's Memorial Building in San Leandro, across the street from Bancroft Middle School.

The guests browsed photo-collages of the graduates' lives like museum exhibits, listened to a master of ceremonies read emotional tributes from their families, and cheered them for their accomplishments.

All were accepted to colleges, and most have athletic scholarships. They have excelled in sports, and many earned honor roll status in high school.

Cheatham was named the "premier African-American male scholar athlete in the nation" this year by the National Alliance of African-American Athletes. Dixon and Stokes were drafted earlier this month by professional baseball teams.

"It feels good to be among all these

See **NINE**, Local 2

"We are doing good things in the world"

► **NINE**, from Local 1

great student athletes" Stokes said. Sometimes young black people are put in groups but there are actually those in a group who are doing good things in the world. Stokes was drafted recently by the Houston Astros. Instead of turning professional, he accepted an athletic scholarship to California State University and plans to study communications while playing baseball. "Then I can have something to fall back on later," he said.

Dixon, who is named to the Parade Magazine All America Football team, has not decided whether he will attend the University of Oregon or sign on with the Cincinnati Reds, he said. But sports were mainly a backdrop Saturday. The focus were on the graduate's personal determination and support they've received from friends, family, and their friends' families.

Dawson's father, James Sr. died three years ago in jail. Authorities said he committed suicide, but family members say he was killed. Dawson's friends helped him grieve and keep going under the emotional strain, he said. "That's how I walked across the stage to graduate last week, and I was so happy" Dawson said. "I did it, and I did it with my friends." Dawson is now headed for Utah State University on a football scholarship. He and his friends took turns with the microphone Saturday thanking their parents for years of cheering them on at sports events, staying after them to do homework, and bearing their financial costs.

And several parents point to a team effort on their part. "They say it takes a village to raise a child, and we've been that village" said McPherson's mother, Juanita Littlejohn. "Any one of these kids can show up at anyone's house and get dinner, spend the night, get a ride, a hug, whatever it takes."

Sunday, Wooldridge heads off to the University of Minnesota for summer classes. Others will leave soon. Even the ones going to nearby schools face new phases in their lives with new challenges ahead.

"We won't let you down" Crosby told the families at long banquet tables. "Because it's hard to fall with all these people behind you."

Jason Bono can be reached at (510) 293-2479 or at jbono@angnewspaper.com

James attended Utah State in his freshman year. He went on to Grambling where he graduated in 2007.

The Investigation

F amily members and friends made an overflow of telephone
calls to Cochran's law firm in Chicago. Attorney Douglas
Hopson was sent to discuss the circumstances surrounding James'
death. When Attorney Hopson arrived at my parents' home on
November 17, 2000, his ears were filled with how James lived his
life, how he was totally against suicide, and how the family saw no
marks on his neck when he was pronounced dead. They even
showed him the photographs Michael had taken of the neck. They
told him Michael asked the nurse in the room why there weren't
any marks on his neck. They told him that two different objects
were claimed to have been used to hang James. I mean, my family
really poured their hearts out to Attorney Hopson.

Attorney Hopson listened then asked a few questions. Mom,
Stevie, and Michael retraced what had occurred repeatedly, until Michael got a pen and paper and wrote everything down. On
November 17, no official documents had yet been received pertaining to James' death—no autopsy reports, no death
certificates, no medical records—nothing had been received
eleven days after his death. The only concrete evidence we had
were the photographs and our gut feelings of a wrongdoing. Of
course, gut feelings don't count for anything. It is only natural
for a family to not want to believe a loved one may have taken
their own life. The allegation presented by a jail staff goes
against a family's gut feelings, the odds are going to be with the
jail staff. What are the odds of a family arriving at the hospital
with the body of an alleged hanging victim? What are the odds
of a family being able to photograph the body in its original
state having no marks on the neck? Those odds just may turn
that family into the favorite, you would think.

Attorney Hopson pulled out his wrongful death contract and
explained it, and Mom signed it. He assured us that if there

were any justice to be found, they would find it. He said they must obtain the object used in the alleged hanging, especially since the photographs Michael took showed no marks on the neck. We explained the emergency room physician initially told us a shower curtain was used then the recording nurse told us a belt; however, two days prior to meeting with Attorney Hopson, we were informed by the investigating officer, Mr. Kelly Hodge, that the official object now was a bed sheet. The three different objects given each leave their own distinctive pattern of marks on the neck.

We told Attorney Hopson about two of James' friends that he had talked to within an hour of being stopped by the police. I gave him a statement from one of them. James told them he was not going to be able to make the trip to Tunica because of a court date he had forgotten about. Attorney Hopson told us he would retrieve the last transactions made from James' cell phone. He had us convinced that he was ready for a war in our fight for justice.

I stayed in contact with Attorney Hopson and continued giving him all of the information I gathered. To me, time was of the essence. I knew most wrongful death cases take months and years, and sometimes justice never prevails. I had already made up my mind that I was not about to let anything get past me. It took Attorney Hopson a couple of months before his initial enthusiasm took a drastic turn for the worse.

In early December, a supporter called Mom to ask for our attorney's name and number because she had information she wanted to share with him. She was a white female who James had tended to her car when she had business in the condos where he worked. She lived in the Mattoon area where James was taken to jail. She knew the coroner and the Springfield pathologist, which I thought was ironic, but I imagine in a small town, everybody knows everybody. She told Mom about an article she read in the local newspaper reporting that James was stopped for drunk driving after leaving a gas station. She asked

Mom if she could attend the coroner's inquest, scheduled to take place on December 20. Mom told her we had not been notified of the proceedings, but that she had no problem with her attending. Mom then gave her our attorney's name and number.

When Mom got off the phone and told me about her conversation, I ignored the allegation of drunk driving because James did not drink. That was just one more lie added to all the rest. When Mom told me James had been seen leaving the gas station the conversation became relevant. As you may recall, when Michael got in James' vehicle, the gas gauge read full, and his vehicle was impound at a gas station, so the dots sort of connected in my mind.

I called Attorney Hopson to tell him about the conversation Mom had and to let him know the woman would be contacting him. I told him about the article she read, and I asked why we had not heard anything about it. He told me it was probably just a part of their investigation and for me not to worry because the autopsy report would reveal the truth. I then asked how the inquest proceedings could be scheduled and advertised in their local newspaper without us being notified. He told me we still had plenty of time to be notified. He then said it really did not make sense for families to attend those proceedings anyway because neither the families nor their attorneys can ask any questions or see any of the evidence being presented. I told Attorney Hopson that anything pertaining to my brother's death was of the utmost importance, no matter what the proceedings were, and especially if it was going to show how they arrived at their suicide verdict.

Sure enough, a few days later, the coroner's inquest notification arrived, only it arrived to the wrong address. It was fortunate the address it had arrived to did exist, and the family knew my family and brought it to my parents' home. I called Attorney Hopson to let him know the notification had arrived, and the manner in which it had arrived. He mildly said that the incorrect address was probably an honest mistake, a typo, perhaps. He then told me that it would cost $700 for him to attend the proceedings, at $100 an hour. We were paying for the three hours it would take him to arrive in Mattoon, an hour for the proceedings, and the three hours it would take him to return to Chicago. I told Attorney Hopson that since he had already told me that neither families nor their attorneys could do anything, we would just let him know what happened. This was not a pro bono case, and we were not expecting anything free, but that was an expensive ride for somebody who was not going to be able to do anything.

The Inquest

December 20 arrived. The coroner's inquest was scheduled for seven p.m. The weather was terrible. Winds blew the snow to where sight was almost impossible. Cars were stranded; some were even swept into the ditches. I prayed as I drove in the hazardous conditions, and my prayers were answered. We arrived to the Mattoon City Hall safely. Due to the bad weather, we arrived to the proceedings at 7:07, hoping they were still in progress. We were the only African-Americans there, and since we had arrived late, it seemed all eyes were on us. We sat down as the investigating officer was giving his testimony. His back was facing us, so he had no idea we were there. Listening to his testimony, I thought we had entered the wrong proceedings because the person he was describing was not my brother. All of a sudden, a man stood and said, "I'm taking a minute recess." I could not understand how he could just stand up in the middle of a person's testimony and take a recess. It's not as if the investigating officer had stopped talking or paused or anything like that; he was still talking. The first thing that came to my mind was the commercial about people with overactive bladders saying, "Gotta go, gotta go, gotta go right now."

When the man left the room, the other jurors stayed in their seats. Moments later, the investigating officer looked our direction and started walking toward us. He approached Mom. He already knew who she was since he interrogated her at the jail the day James died. He introduced himself to the rest of the family then said, "I did not think you were going to make it."

I said, "I guess no one thought we were going to make it since the inquest notification was sent to the wrong address."

He looked at me as if he had no idea what I was talking about. He then told us that we had not missed too much, and as soon as the proceedings were over, we should feel free to ask any question we had. I don't know if this was an exception to the rules, but this proceeding was nothing as our attorney said it would be.

Moments later, the man returned from his recess, and the proceedings continued. I noticed the investigating officer's testimony was not as strong as it was before he knew we were present. Then it struck me that the sudden request for the minute recess was to let the investigating officer know that the family of James Dawson was in the house, so to be very cautious throughout the remainder of his testimony. After the investigating officer's testimony ended, the unanimous suicide verdict was read, and that was the end of the investigation into the death of James Dawson. No one challenged the verdict.

When the proceedings ended, we did not give the investigating officer a chance to come back to us—we went over to him. I asked whom the man was that took the recess in the middle of his testimony. He told me that was the coroner. I asked what the recess was for. He told me he had no idea. As soon as I knew it was the coroner, my curiosity shifted into high gear because the coroner was also the one who told Mom it was the law to have James' body transported to Springfield, which is where they got rid of all his organs and brain. I had talked to him on two occasions and asked why there were no marks on James' neck. He'd boldly evaded the question both times. I had to restrain myself and continue with my many questions. The investigating officer started to gather his things and I asked if I could see the photograph of the shower curtain rod James had allegedly hanged himself on. You see, all this time, I was thinking since we were dealing with a hanging, that it took place on a pole in the ceiling or something. However, it was not a pole, but a shower curtain rod. As I looked at the photograph, I asked if there was a shower curtain hanging from the rod. He told me no. I asked the purpose of the shower curtain rod. He told me he had no idea. I asked if there were curtain rods without shower curtains in other cells. He told me his investigation centered on the cell James occupied. I asked if the curtain rod was in open view, if a person lying down or sitting in the cell could see it. He told me a person would have to step inside the shower because the rod was behind a block wall. Therefore, James had to step inside the shower area, look above the shower entrance where no shower curtain was hanging to locate this shower curtain rod.

The next photograph was of a pair of sandals. One sandal was at the door entrance of the shower and the other was at the drainage of the shower. They were spread apart. I asked what that photograph was for. He told me it was a picture of the sandals James had kicked off his feet during the hanging. Why would someone intending to hang himself even think about putting on sandals when he already had socks on his feet? The investigating officer actually lost me with that one, because according to his own statement during the proceedings, James was found partially hanging, his feet resting on the floor, and he could have stood up. But with one sandal at the entrance and the other at the drainage, they appeared to have been kicked off the feet of someone suspended in midair. After reviewing the two photographs there was no more I wanted to say. I concluded by asking if I could have a copy of the two photographs. He gave me the name and number of Ms. Maryland Huckaby for any requests. Walking away, I asked if there were any other people processed on the night of November 5. He looked at his notes and told me there were seven other people. I asked if they were all white. He told me they were, but that this was not a race issue because James was in a cell by himself. I told him I was not trying to make it a race issue, I just need to be aware of all the circumstances surrounding my brother's death.

As we were leaving the Mattoon City Hall, the supporter who called Mom for our attorney's name and number introduced herself. We hugged and prayed that someday justice would prevail. The supporter shared her fondest memories of James, then continued with how very disappointed she was in the way our attorney was handling the case. She said he did not have a positive attitude about the case. He believed James took his own life. She said when she told him she would be attending the proceedings, he asked her to take notes for him. I don't know if our attorney thought we would not be attending, or if he had completely lost his mind by asking her to take notes for him as if she was his private secretary. I was embarrassed on his behalf as a professional representing us. He could have told us he did not believe in our wrongful death claim, and he could have easily requested a copy of the coroner's inquest in its entirety as I had, instead of stooping to those measures. After we departed the Mattoon City Hall, we had no further contact with the supporter. I hand delivered a copy of the coroner's inquest to our attorney's office.

This is the request sent to Ms. Maryland Huckaby, followed by the denial from freedom of information:

Dear Ms. Maryland Huckaby:

Upon our telephone conversation on 1/11/01, you informed me that I need to send to you in writing my request. Here is my request in writing. On December 20, 2000 there was a Coroner's inquest proceedings held at the Mattoon City Hall at 7:00 p.m. in the cause of death for James Dawson. After the proceedings I talked to investigating officer Kelly Hodge and he gave me your name and number to contact for any requests I may have. During the proceedings there were two photographs shown that I would like a copy of if at all possible. One photograph is of the shower curtain rod James allegedly hanged himself on, and the other photograph is of a pair of sandals. One sandal is at the drainage of the shower and the other is at the entrance of the shower.

In addition to the two photographs, I would like the name of the arresting officer who stopped the vehicle of James Dawson on the night of November 5, 2000 at 11:20 p.m. on I – 57 and took him to the Cumberland County jail for detainment for being caught while driving on a suspended license. I talked to a representative from the Office of the Secretary of State, and according to their records, they show NO citation was issued to James Dawson on the night of November 5, 2000. Therefore the name of the arresting officer would be greatly appreciated. Thank you for any assistance you are able to provide to me at this time.

Sincerely,

FREEDOM OF INFORMATION APPEAL
STATE OF ILLINOIS (2)

3486

Date Appeal Received In State Agency

INSTRUCTIONS:
Requestor should fill out sections — DESCRIPTION OF RECORDS, and REASONS FOR APPEALING. Send copies 1 and 2 to the Director of the Agency which original request was sent to. Unless notified otherwise the Agency's response will be within 7 working days after receipt of appeal.

Requestor's Name (Or business name if applicable)
Margaret (Dawson) Brown

Send Appeal To: (Director and Agency)
Illinois State Police

Street Address

Street Address
201 East Adams, Suite 100

City
Chicago

State
Illinois

Zip

City
Springfield

State
Illinois

Zip
62701

DESCRIPTION OF RECORDS THAT APPEAL IS BEING MADE FOR:

1.) A copy of two photographs shown by investigating officer Kelly Hodge at the Coroner's inquest proceedings held on December 20, 2000 at the Mattoon City Hall at 7:00 p.m. in the cause of death for James Dawson. One photograph is of the shower curtain rod James Dawson allegedly hanged himself on, and the other photograph is of a pair of sandals. One sandal is at the door entrance of the shower and the other sandal is at the drainage of the shower.

2.) A copy of the traffic citation issued to James Dawson as he was stopped for speeding and driving on a suspended license on the night of December 5, 2000.

REASONS FOR APPEALING

For Personal Investigation.

DIRECTOR'S RESPONSE TO APPEAL

Noted below is the action I have taken on your appeal from the denial of your request for the above captioned records

[ ] I hereby approve your appeal to the following extent and for the following reasons:

[X] I affirm the denial of your request made by the Freedom of Information Officer.

Note: You are entitled to judicial review of any denial pursuant to Section II of the Freedom of Information Act.

The information required by this form is MANDATORY in order to comply with P.A. 83-1013. Failure to so provide may result in this form not being processed. This form is approved by the Forms Management Center.

Director's Signature

Date of Reply
02-08-01

L 001-0006 (6/84)
LEGEND FOR REQUESTOR: 1st copy (white) - send to Agency; 2nd copy (canary) - send to Agency; 3rd copy (pink) - Requestor's copy

I wanted to gather as much incriminating evidence as I could. Eight months into my investigation, I thought about the article the supporter told Mom about that we never got to see. Unfortunately, looking for the article was like looking for a needle in a haystack. I made a few telephone calls and was told I should be able to locate the article in the Springfield library. I drove to Springfield from Chicago, a six-hour trip—three hours there and three hours back. Once I arrived at the Springfield library, I just knew I had it made, but looking through the tiny microfilms, not knowing the exact date or newspaper the article was printed in, made my search difficult. After James' autopsy provided proof that toxicology was negative for drugs or alcohol, the article was demeaning of character. More importantly, someone had to release the story in order for it to have been printed. Although I was unsuccessful in locating that article, I did locate this one, which was printed on November 9, 2000, three days after James death:

Toledo:
Man reportedly hangs himself in county jail.

A Chicago man dies from injuries sustained when he apparently hung himself in a cell at the Cumberland County jail. James Dawson 37 was found hanging by a sheet late Monday morning said police Master Sgt. Jerry Pea. Dawson was taken to the Sarah Bush Lincoln Health Center where he was pronounced dead by Coles County Coroner Mike Nichols. Pea said Dawson was alone in the cell when the incident occurred and there is no signs of foul play. Pea said the investigation continues.

COPY OF THE CORONER'S INQUEST PROCEEDINGS:

```
                    CORONER INQUEST
              INTO THE CAUSE OF DEATH
                  OF JAMES DAWSON
```

```
              BE IT REMEMBERED that on the 20th day
     of December, A.D., 2000 the following proceedings
     were conducted at Mattoon City Hall, Mattoon,
     Illinois, upon the inquest into the death of
     JAMES DAWSON.
```

```
                  Gary J. Maninfior
                     CSR #84-573
     ---------------------------------------------------
     M A N I N F I O R   C O U R T   R E P O R T I N G


                CERTIFIED SHORTHAND REPORTERS
                       1612 Lafayette
                     P.  O.  Box 1036
                 Mattoon, Illinois  61938
                      800-346-2986
```

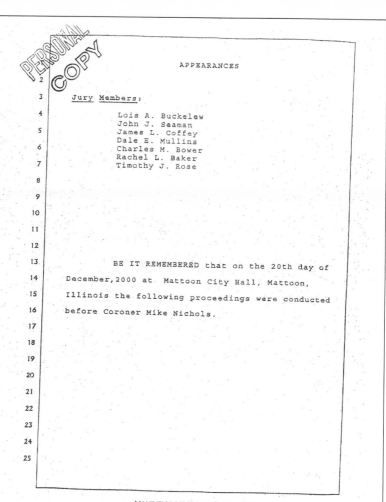

APPEARANCES

Jury Members:

Lois A. Buckelew
John J. Seaman
James L. Coffey
Dale E. Mullins
Charles M. Bower
Rachel L. Baker
Timothy J. Rose

        BE IT REMEMBERED that on the 20th day of December, 2000 at Mattoon City Hall, Mattoon, Illinois the following proceedings were conducted before Coroner Mike Nichols.

MANINFIOR REPORTING SERVICE, P.C.
1-800-346-2986

78

Coroner Nichols: Okay, ladies and gentlemen of the jury, you have got a paper there in front of you and hopefully a paper and pen to write with and take notes. You will need to get it to write down the date, time and location of death and all the particulars as you go through the proceedings that will be pertinent to the verdict.

Okay, we've got two cases we will be hearing tonight. The first one is that of James Dawson, age thirty-seven (37) of Chicago who was brought to Sarah Bush Lincoln Health Center where he was pronounced dead at 1:05 p.m. on November 7th. He had been traversed by Toledo Ambulance from the Cumberland County Jail where he was an inmate down there. He was discovered hanging by the neck by a bed sheet in his jail cell.

The other case is that of Judith Cook, age forty-four (44) of Martinsville, a passenger in an automobile driven by her mother, Mildred Cook. She was involved in a vehicle accident on the Clarksville and (Klein Orchard Drive intersection ands both were transported by Westfield Ambulance to Sarah Bush Lincoln Health Center.

Judith was pronounced dead in the emergency room on November 14th at 10:19 a.m.

Will the jury please stand and raise your right hand?

(At this point in the proceedings the jurors were first duly sworn upon their her oath, after which the following proceedings were conducted:

Coroner Nichols: Okay, ladies and gentlemen of the jury and others present, this is an inquest of James Dawson, black male, age thirty-seven (37)   of Chicago, Illinois. At about 11:20 on November 5th he was stopped for speeding on I-57. When they ran a driver's license check on him they found out his license had been suspended. He was arrested at that time and transported to the Cumberland County Jail pending bond of one hundred dollars ($100.00) and then on November 6th at approximately 11:30 a.m. his family arrived at the jail with the bail. At 11:50 Deputy Cornell went to Mr. Dawson and found him hanging or partially suspended hanging from a bed sheet in the shower stall. This was in his cell. She summoned Sheriff Sowers and Chief Deputy McCord and they

came to his assistance and got Mr. Dawson down and
started CPR. Then in turn called the ambulance
and they took over upon their arrival and then he
was transported to Sarah Bush and life support was
administered in route. Once he got to the
hospital they were unable to revive him and he was
officially pronounced dead at 1:05 p.m. A
forensic autopsy was performed at 7:30 the
following morning. The cause of death was hanging
by the neck with partial suspension.
In other words, when we're talking about partial
suspension he could have stood up and stopped his
death or the suffocation in the bed sheet that was
tied around his neck.

Okay, toxicology was drawn and
analyzed and it was totally negative to any drugs
or alcohol in his system.

This is neither a civil nor a criminal
proceeding, just a matter into the inquest
inquiring into this man's death.

I call forward Kelly Hodge of the
Illinois State Police, District 9 of Effingham in
this matter.

KELLY HODGE

The witness having been first duly sworn

upon his oath testified as follows:

EXAMINATION CONDUCTED

BY: Coroner Nichols

Q.   Tell us for the record your name and occupation.

A.   My name is Kelly Hodge. I'm a special agent with the Illinois State Police.

Q.   Kelly, where did this death occur?

A.   He was pronounced dead at Sarah Bush Hospital.

Q.   And when did this incident happen?

A.   It was on November 6th at approximately 11:50 a.m. he was discovered.

Q.   I basically told the jury what partial suspension was, would you go ahead and describe that in your own words?

A.   This is as it was described to me by Correctional Officer Cornell, female working the jail, and also she was the one who initially discovered Mr. Dawson. She said when she walked into the cell he was partially suspended by a bed sheet that was tied onto a shower curtain rod and then again around his neck and his legs had a slight bend to them, and she commented to me that he could have stood up and she didn't understand

Also, Sheriff Houser after she discovered the body she ran back to the jail and summoned the sheriff and chief deputy and they came back to the cell and found Mr. Dawson suspended by the bed sheet around the shower curtain rod and they felt like at that time that there was a chance they could revive him, so they took him down as quickly as possible and started CPR.

Q.   His jail cell, is it isolated from any other prisoners or were there any other prisoners in any lock up, at that time?

A.   No, he had a cell to himself and had been secured there approximately 2:00 to 2:30 a.m. on the 6th and was never taken out of the cell again after that and no one entered his cell after that until Mrs. Cornell, or Correctional Officer Cornell discovered him.

Q.   Okay, was the bed sheet he used that was in his own bunk then?

A.   Correct, he was issued that bed sheet as well as some other linens. When he became confined in the jail they issued these items to him.

71

Q. He had on a jail uniform then, is that correct?

A. Yes, and forgive my artistic abilities, but there is another copy there. This is of the cell itself.

Q. You want to start this around to the jury?

A. All right, this is of the cell, the doors at the very bottom as it faces you. That is the only entrance to the cell. And you will see on there the cell, I would say I did not take a measurement of it, but it is approximately 12x14, a relatively good-sized cell. There is different levels of security and different types of cells. It has a telephone, sink and toilet and shower and also had its own pay telephone in it. The jail doesn't, as I understand, doesn't have a strict policy on who gets these cells, but if they have someone that will be there for a relatively short period of time and also someone who has given them no problems, been an otherwise good person and is going to be there a short time, they do get a slightly better arrangement and that was the case with Mr. Dawson also.

Q. This shower rod shown in this drawing

here that is where he hung himself?

A.   Yes, that is correct.

Q.   That is right around -- now this front wall here, is that a block wall or is that bars?

A.   That is a block wall. The only way that you can see into the cell there is a small window approximately head high and there is a small door, I believe they call it a food port, that you can open up the door and slide the food tray through so you don't have to open up the door to feed someone, and when that food port is open, which is left open pretty much all the time because it makes it easier on correctional officers, especially when they are not very tall, they can look into the cell and check and look straight to the bed, which is clearly visible and they can often times check on the inmate at that time when they do the cell check.

Q.   Their normal cell check time is roughly half hour increments?

A.   Yes, that varies depending on how many they have working and how many people are in the jail. Sometimes they can be slightly longer or slightly shorter, but they shoot for thirty minutes.

Q.   Now in this cell here out of the outer
corridor leading to the various other cells there
there is a survey lens camera I understand?

A.   That is correct.

Q.   Do you have some drawings on that you
can pass around?

A.   Yes, this one is basically a
continuation of the drawing that you have. It
will start at the door to the cell and travel back
out into the booking area. I'll pass it out first
and explain it.

To orientate so you can read the
wording what you will see is a hall to Mr.
Dawson's cell; that is the hallway that is
captured on the security camera; this is, this
main area is called the booking area, from this
booking area if you travel down the hallway
approximately twenty feet you would go back to Mr.
Dawson's cell that he was at. The security camera
does not capture the incident and does not capture
the door to the cell. What it captures is the
doorway going to that cell, and as I understand it
that is the only entrance to there. There is an
outside exit, but to access this cell you have to
go through the booking area.

Q.   So there is no other way, is there, to
his cell, other than through this?

A.   No.

Q.   And these other cells here, they are in
plain view then? This is just a three cell jail?

A.   In this portion, yes. This is one wing
or one section of the Cumberland County Jail.
There is other cells, other parts of the jail. To
make it clear he was the only person in his cell.
There was one other person in that area in one of
the other cells. It was unclear at the time which
cell he was in, but he was a trustee and he helped
feed other prisoners. In fact, he fed Mr. Dawson
earlier that morning.

Q.   And he appeared to be all right
at that time?

A.   Yes, that was approximately 7:00 or
7:30 a.m.

Juror: What time was that?

A.   Let me double check the time on that.
Approximately 7:30 and Auddie Decker, the trustee,
advised that he fed breakfast to Mr. Dawson
through the food port.

Mr. Decker also testified at a, well,
correction, he didn't testify, gave me a statement

that he again saw Mr. Dawson at approximately
11:05 a.m. This is corroborated by the security
camera. It shows Mr. Decker walking to a cell or
bathroom area and in your map of the booking area
you will see off to the right-hand side it says
"door to bathroom." On the video Mr. Decker is
captured standing at that door looking down the
hallway to Mr. Dawson's cell. At that time he
says the food port was open and he could see into
the cell. He could see the bunk and see Mr.
Dawson laying on his bunk. He didn't know if he
was asleep.

This will make it a little clearer. I
do have some photos of the cell area. In fact, I
stood at the, you can pass this down. I don't
have a copy for everybody. This first photo, if
you could take a look. What you're seeing is the
view that Mr. Decker had in the jail standing out
the door to the bathroom. Just before he enters
you see on the video, him opening up the door to
his left looking down the hallway, which is only a
matter of fifteen to twenty feet to the cell and
he said at 11:05 a.m. he saw Mr. Dawson laying on
his bunk.

Q.   These videos are all time marked then?

A. Yes, they are.

Q. So that is all corroborated actually on video then?

A. Yes, Mr. Decker says at 11:05. According to the video it was 11:08.

Q. So approximately then?

A. Yes. Also this small picture like that don't capture, since it is so small it doesn't capture exactly what you would see if you were standing there. The food port is six or eight inches by five so when you're standing there you can clearly see into the cell or a bunk, or if someone is laying there you can see them. The food port in this picture is so small it appears that you couldn't see in there, but you can.

These next pictures are interior shots of the cell area. They basically show the interior of the cell including the shower area. These are just different shots of the cell itself and to give you kind of an idea of what it looked like

Q. I'll give everybody a chance to review the pictures. While we are looking at the pictures at any time that you feel you need to ask a question please feel free to ask it, that is what we are here for, to make sure everybody understands what took place.

Juror: Did he have any previous discussion as far as prior to -- that he may have an idea he might do something like this?

A.   The only indication, if you will, the arresting officer that night who stopped him for speeding and arrested him when he first stopped the vehicle -- Cumberland County Sheriff's office, when he spoke with Mr. Dawson he asked him where he was going to. He said he was just out driving, and keep in mind he lives in Chicago, a couple hundred miles. He didn't have a destination in mind.

The officer stated that he was nervous, but that is not uncommon of someone getting stopped by a police officer, but he did tell him that he needed to talk to somebody and the officer asked him "What do you mean? Are you talking about a counselor or what do you mean"? He said "No, you will do", and he told him that he and his wife were separated. That was really the only other indication that there was anything on his mind or that he was upset about anything.

Everyone else at the jail said that he

was a nice pleasant man; didn't seem to be depressed or upset about anything; and naturally he wasn't overly excited about being in the Cumberland County Jail, but there was no indication that he was upset or depressed, other than the one comment he made.

Juror: Do you know approximately how tall he was?

A. I'm not sure of the height. I think approximately, this is an approximate. Height I think approximately 5'8" to 5'9". I think approximately between two twenty (220) and two forty (240).

Mrs. Dawson (Deceased's mother): I would say he was about one hundred eighty or ninety

A. I can look at the pathology report to find that for you.

Juror: How tall is the bar in the shower?

A. It is a little over 6'3", 6'4", right around there. I'm six foot, I can reach up and grab the bar easily. In fact, since we are talking abou the bar, I weigh approximately between one ninety-five and two hundred pounds,

and I suspended my weight from the bar and easily
held that weight and it is done that way for a
reason, for security reasons for the jail. If you
have a bar that could easily be pulled down it
could be used as a weapon, so they make these
sturdy enough and they bolt them into the wall
with heavy bolts so they will not come down. It
showed no sign of my two hundred pounds when I was
holding onto it of coming down or bending. It is
very sturdy.

Juror: Is the telephone in the room,
are they pay telephones?

A.   Yes, they are pay telephones in his
room, yes.

Q.   I didn't see anything in the pathology
report as to the weight of the individual.

A.   Okay. I would trust Mrs. Dawson of his
height and weight.

The last photo I have, you can pass
this around. This would be the top; that is
standing inside; that is standing inside the
shower stall looking back up behind you, if you
will, to the shower curtain rod and it is just to
give you an idea, a stainless steel rod.

I found in the records based on his

drivers license and also his booking on the
check-in sheet at the jail it shows 5'6" one
hundred seventy-five. That is on the driver's
license. That could vary slightly in weight and
height.

Q. Right. On your observation and your
investigation you have pretty well determined that
through all the records and the reviewing the
videotapes that there was no other individual
involved in this whatsoever?

A. My investigation did not show any
indication that anybody else entered that cell and
that is--

Q. And the video tape corroborates all of
this?

A. Yes, that is true. The videotape shows
with slight variation in times, Mr. Decker, like I
said was off by a couple of minutes. Other than
that the times are relatively close, within a few
minutes of each other. The last correctional
officer, Deborah Cornell, was the last one to see
him and that was at 11:20 a.m. and she was in the
kitchen area. You will notice at the bottom of
your drawing where it says, there is an arrow that
says "to kitchen" that is an open area and it is

relatively wide, approximately ten to fifteen feet
wide.   If you're standing in the kitchen area you
can see through this.   It is an open area, but it
is separated by bars.   You can see all the way
down the hall to Mr. Dawson's cell from that area.
And Mrs. Cornell said that she, at 11:20, was in
the kitchen area delivering groceries and looked
down there and could see him laying on his bunk
at that time and he wasn't again found until
11:50.   There was a twenty minute period there.

I would comment there I did attend the
autopsy with Doctor Heimann from Springfield and
he put in his report also, and I observed no
trauma to Mr. Dawson whatsoever.   There was a mark
on his chin, underneath his chin, that was earlier
at the hospital and possibly by some of the
emergency medical people reported as an abrasion.
At the autopsy I asked the pathologist to explain
this abrasion and he quickly corrected me and said
is was not an abrasion, but a pressure mark and he
said the mark occurred due to the ligature or
sheet that was around Mr. Dawson's neck and had
absolutely nothing to do with the death of Mr.
Dawson and was not an injury, so to speak, that it
was caused by the sheet.

Q.   Actually it was left as a postmortem mark then?

A.   Yes.

Q.   That was about where the knot was tied then apparently?

A.   I did not see the knot, of course.

Q.   They took it down immediately when they found him?

A.   Yes.

Juror: How was it secured, the knot?

A.   The knot was tied over the shower curtain rod and then around his neck. Normally we would want to preserve those knots, but when the sheriff and chief deputy came into the cell their first and immediate reaction was to get him down and the sheriff told me that he thought he felt warm to the touch and if they started CPR he felt they might be able to save him and the last thing on their mind was preserving the knot.

Juror: What was he stopped for?

A.   Speeding, southbound just north of the Neoga exit, mile post 179.

Juror: Why he was taken in? Why wasn't he just given a ticket?

A.   He was not taken in for speeding.

...e able to post bond or your driver's license
... a speeding offense, but when they checked his
driver's license it was suspended and for an
offense of that nature normally you have to post
bond, and the only place you can post bond is at
the jail.

Q.   And he did not have bail money on him,
is that correct?

A.   No, he needed one hundred dollars and
he did not have that much on him.

Q.   And, again, the reason for his family
coming down there then was to post bond?

A.   Yes.

Q.   If he had not had his license suspended
he would not have been taken into the jail?

A.   Correct, had it not been suspended he
could have posted bond with a driver's license or
even his signature could have been used as a bond.

Coroner Nichols: Anything further you
want to bring into the testimony?

A.   Earlier there was a question by one of
the jurors what his state of mind was, whether he
was upset or anything and the only other statement
that I got was from another correctional officer
who was working the midnight shift who also backed

the other people and said that he was a very nice, pleasant person and wished all the people they dealt with was like that. When they were conversing, when they took Mr. Dawson out of the cell because he was trying to make a collect call and he couldn't make a collect call from the cell and they took him to the booking area and let him use the county telephone. During that time they talked and they asked him if he was married and Mr. Dawson said, kind of chuckled and said "Yeah, on paper." So it was also another backing up what he had said previously about being separated from his wife, or at least separate living arrangements.

> Q.   Where is his wife at now then?

> A.   She is in Chicago. She was also contacted, by the way. She could not provide any information.

> Q.   As to why either?

> A.   Right.

> Juror: Didn't want to or-

> A.   She provided a statement, but she didn't have any insight, didn't have any information as to where he was going on that night. She couldn't understand why he was that

far south of Chicago, but she said that she
wouldn't know of any reason why he or someone else
would do this. She didn't have any information
whatsoever, but she did confirm that they were
living apart.

   Juror: Did they have an argument that
night or something?

  A. No, not that she would state. There
was no indication of that whatsoever. I believe
that's all I have to add unless somebody has a
question.

   Coroner Nichols: Do you have any other
questions of this witness? You may step down
then. Thank you.

   Okay, the date and time of death of
Mr. Dawson was on November 6th at 1:05 p.m. at
Sarah Bush Lincoln Health Center.

   Juror: 1:05 did you say?

   Coroner Nichols: Yes.

   Juror: On the 7th?

  A. On the 6th.

   Juror: On the 7th? Excuse me, it was
1:07 on the --

  A. 1:05 p.m. on the 7th.

   Juror: He was found November 6th.

Coroner Nichols: He was stopped on the 6th. And the cause of death was hanging by the neck with partial suspension and he used the bed sheet for that purpose and then it was determined whether anybody else was involved or not and it was indicated that there was not.

Any final questions before you go in to deliberate then on your verdict? Okay, ladies and gentlemen of the jury, this constitutes the evidence available. It is now your duty to deliver the findings and if possible to arrive at a verdict as to cause of death, whether you deem it to be accidental, unavoidable, avoidable, suicidal, homicidal, premeditated or manslaughter or undetermined, and whether the blame should be placed on anyone concerned. When you have reached a verdict you will deliver to me, the Coroner of Coles County, to the best of your belief.

You will have all of this evidence to ponder over for your verdict.

(At approximately 7:37 the jurors left to deliberate, returning at approximately 7:55, after which the following proceedings were conducted:)

Coroner Nichols: Okay, ladies and

lemen of the jury, have you reached a verdict?
uld the foreman please read from the top down,
read the verdict?

       Foreman: From here?

       Coroner Nichols: Yes.

       Foreman: In the matter of the inquest
on the body of James Dawson, deceased, held at
Mattoon, County of Coles, State of Illinois on the
20th day of December 2000, we the jurors inquiring
into the death, on oath do find he came to his
death by hanging by the neck, partial suspension.
We, the jury, do concur that James Dawson died at
Sarah Bush Lincoln Hospital at 1:05 p.m. on
November 6, 2000 due to suicide.

       Coroner Nichols: Do the rest of the
jurors agree with this verdict?

       (All answer affirmatively)

       Coroner Nichols: The matter is
therefore closed of James Dawson.

CERTIFIED SHORTHAND REPORTER'S CERTIFICATION

2

3   I, GARY J. MANINFIOR, Certified
    Shorthand Reporter and Notary Public of the State
    of Illinois, do hereby certify that on the 20th
4   day of December, A.D., 2000 I did take
    stenographic notes of the inquest of JAMES DAWSON
5   and that said notes were reduced to typewritten
    form under my direction and supervision.

6

7   I do further certify that the attached
    and foregoing is a true, correct, and complete
8   copy of my notes and that said testimony is now
    herewith returned.

9

10   I do further certify that the said
    deposition was taken at Mattoon City Hall,
11 Mattoon, Illinois.

12

13   I do further certify that I am not
    related in any way to any of the parties involved
    in this action and have no interest in the outcome
14 thereof.

15

16   Dated at Mattoon, Illinois this 28th day
    of December, A.D., 2000 and given under my hand
    and seal.

17

18

19 _____
         Gary J. Maninfior, Reporter
20

21

22

23

24

25

MANINFIOR REPORTING SERVICE, P.C.
1-800-346-2986

Immediately following the coroner's inquest, I requested a copy of the proceedings in writing. I did not receive the copy until January 21, 2001. Since we arrived seven minutes late, we missed part of the "show." What we did witness was more than enough. Reading the proceedings in its entirety is breathtaking because there is much that we would never have known about, even after attending the proceedings. I really would like to look through the eyes of the investigating officer and those seven white jurors to see exactly what they had seen to come to a suicide verdict. I don't think they ever imagined their vision would be re-examined so very thoroughly. Unfortunately, this isn't *Murder, She Wrote,* in which the guilty parties are always revealed. This is just a case of solid evidence presented by James Dawson's family and friends that sometimes a suicide hanging is not what it is set up to be. Here is my refutation:

Refutation

In the introduction, the inquest transcript stated, "Okay we have got two cases we will be hearing tonight. The first one is that of James Dawson, age thirty seven of Chicago, who was brought to the Sarah Bush Lincoln Health Center where he was pronounced dead at 1:05 p.m. on November 7th. He had been traversed by the Toledo Ambulance from Cumberland County jail where he was an inmate down there."

*** Actually, he was pronounced dead at 1:05 p.m. on November 6. As far as him being an inmate, he was taken to jail for driving on a suspended license, and if that means he was an inmate then I guess he was an inmate. ***

The transcript stated, "At approximately 11:30 a.m., his family arrived at the jail with the bail. At 11:50 Deputy Cornell went to Mr. Dawson and found him hanging or partially hanging from a bed sheet in the shower stall in his cell."

The transcript stated, "She summoned Sheriff Sowers and Chief Deputy McCord, and they came to the assistance and got Mr. Dawson down and started CPR.

Then in turn, [they] called the ambulance, and [the paramedics] took over upon their arrival. [James] was transported to Sarah Bush Lincoln Health Center, and life support was administered in route. At the hospital, they were unable to revive him, and he was officially pronounced dead at 1:05 p.m. A forensic autopsy was performed at 7:30 a.m. the following morning. The cause of death was hanging by the neck with partial suspension. In other words, he could have stood up and stopped his death or the suffocation in the bed sheet that was tied around his neck. Toxicology was drawn and analyzed and it was totally negative for any drugs or alcohol in his system."

The transcript stated, "He had a cell to himself and had been secured there [at] approximately 2:00 to 2:30 a.m. on the 6th, never taken out of the cell after that, and no one entered the cell until Correctional Officer Cornell discovered him. He was issued the bed sheet as well as some other linen. They issue these items when you are confined to the jail. He had a jail uniform then, is that correct? – Yes."

*** Why was James issued a jail uniform when his only crime was a suspended license? ***

The transcript stated, "What was he stopped for? Speeding. Why was he taken in, and why wasn't he just given a ticket? He was not taken in for speeding. You are able to post bond on your license for a speeding offense, but when they checked James' license it was suspended, and for an offense of that nature, normally you have to post bond, and the only place you can post bond is at the jail."

***The transcript never stated that James had any warrants, or that he had provided no proof of insurance or vehicle registration, was stopped for drunk driving, or anything else. His only crime was speeding and having a suspended license. ***

When my family was escorted back to the jail, Mom was given James' belongings in a clear plastic bag and a yellow, sealed envelope that supposedly contained the currency James had in his possession. Weeks after my brother's death, I decided to go through the plastic bag. I pulled out his black leather jacket. As I went through the pockets, I found a folded Cumberland County detention document. When I read the document, I realized James had been stripped of his clothes and issued a prison uniform for driving on a suspended license. All I could do was wonder how this had happened to my brother. How could he have been driving freely along the expressway, only to be stopped and taken to where death waited right around the corner? How could he have escaped jail all his life, only to lose his life in there for a traffic violation? It's not as if James had planned to go to jail; his destination had been different. If it had been up to James, he would have chosen to die another day. This was his first experience behind the walls of a prison, and unfortunately, it was the last experience of his life. You may now review the detention document:

CUMBERLAND COUNTY DETENTION CENTER
PERSONAL PROPERTY RECEIPT AND RELEASE FORM
166 Courthouse Square
Toledo, Illinois 62468
(217) 849-2312
Fax (217) 849-2519

BASKET # 5   DATE: 11-5-00

NAME: Dawson, James   BOOKING # 0217-00-D

The following items were removed from the above named person.
(Fully describe each article)

QUANTITY	ARTICLES	DATE AND TIME RELEASED
1	yellow watch	
1	yellow coin	
1	pipe	
1	Blue pouch - contents on back	
1	yellow papers	
1	Blue Pants	
1	Blue shirt	
1	shoes - white	

I certify that the above is correct and that any of my properties **NOT CLAIMED** within 6 months of my release will be disposed of by Cumberland County Detention Center.

_____   _____
Detainee's Signature   Officer's Signature

I hereby authorize the Cumberland County Detention Center to release my personal property as indicated above by the date shown to the following person.

_____   _____
Name   Signature of Person Releasing Item(s) and Date

_____   _____
Detainee's Signature and Date   Releasing Officer's Signature

I certify that I have received all of the above listed personal property (minus any property which has been released at an early date and time) on this _____ day of _____ 19_____ at _____ am/pm.

_____   _____
Detainee's Signature   Releasing Officer's Signature

_____   _____
Officer's Signature   County

93

17 - cards
1 - DL suspended
pictures

CUMBERLAND COUNTY DETENTION CENTER
PROPERTY ISSUED AND RETURNED

ITEM	NUMBER OF ITEM AND DATE ISSUED	NUMBER OF ITEM AND DATE RETURNED	CONDITION
BLANKET	11-5-00		
PILLOW COVER			
SHIRT			
PANTS			
SANDALS			
MATTRESS COVER			
TOWEL			
WASHCLOTH	11-5-00		

ITEMS IN CELL AT ALL TIMES: (1) MATTRESS; (1) PILLOW

ISSUED SIGNATURES

_____   _____
DETAINEE'S SIGNATURE   OFFICER'S SIGNATURE

RELEASING SIGNATURES

_____   _____
DETAINEE'S SIGNATURE   OFFICER'S SIGNATURE

Printed in Toledo, Illinois by Homestead Press @ 217 849-3711

The eight items listed that were taken away are:

1. Yellow watch
2. Yellow coin
3. Phone
4. Black pouch (contents on back)
5. Yellow earring
6. Black pants
7. Black shirt
8. Pr. Shoes (white)

When you take these eight items away, what's left? Socks, underwear, and T-shirt perhaps? James was even stripped of an earring from his ear. I wondered why the black leather jacket wasn't listed as one of the items taken.

Items issued are:
1. Blanket
2. Pillow cover
3. Shirt
4. Pants
5. Sandals
6. Mattress cover
7. Towel
8. Washcloth
*Items in cell at all times (1) Mattress (1) Pillow

If these were all the items issued to James, then where is the bed sheet, the object the jail staff claimed they witnessed around James' neck? I don't see a bed sheet listed. How about you? Perhaps a mattress cover and a bed sheet are one and the same; that is debatable.

The date 11-5-00 is written next to "blanket" at the top of the detention sheet and next to washcloth at the bottom of the detention sheet, which verifies that James was issued these items before midnight. He was stopped at 11:20 p.m., and within forty minutes was stripped of his clothes and personal belongings.

When I opened the yellow, sealed envelope, there was only $64.78 inside it. Conveniently, the detention sheet does not list the amount of currency taken away. I'm sure there should have been some kind of document James had to sign to verify the amount of currency he had in his possession. On the detention sheet is listed seventeen cards. There were seventeen cards, as documented, but none of the cards was a credit card or an ATM card, and since James was headed for Tunica, Mississippi, to gamble only having $64.78 sounds unrealistic.

The transcript stated, "And he did not have bail money on him, is that correct? No, he needed one hundred dollars, and he did not have that much on him."

*** The investigating officer knew about the $64.78 inside the sealed envelope. When James talked to Mom, he told her they would not let him post his own bond. That is why he had to have someone come to the jail. He would have told Mom he did not have bail money on him. Regardless of how much money James had in his possession, it didn't matter because the investigating officer stated, "You are able to post bond for a speeding offense, but when they checked James' license, it was suspended." James could not post his own bond on a suspended license. It stated on the detention sheet "1-DL (driver's license) suspended." James did not have his driver's license on him. He was driving on a ticket. What he had on him was his state I.D., not his driver's license. ***

The transcript stated, "They took Mr. Dawson out of the cell because he was trying to make a collect call and he could not do so from the cell so they took him into the booking area to use the county telephone."

*** James was processed before midnight, so why did it take over two hours for him to make a phone call? First, what is up with the pay telephone being inside the cell James occupied, when all his currency was taken before he entered the cell? He had his own cell phone in his possession, so he could have easily called Mom from his cell phone before he was processed and placed inside the cell. ***

When the investigating officer passed around the drawings of the cell and asked the jurors to forgive his artistic abilities, he said, "This is the cell. The doors at the very bottom, as it faces you. That is the only entrance to the cell." He then stated, "You will see the hall to Mr. Dawson's cell; that is the hallway captured on the security camera. This area is called the booking area. From the booking area, if you traveled down the hallway approximately twenty feet, you would go back to Mr. Dawson's cell. The security camera does not capture the incident and does not capture the cell. What it does capture is the doorway going to the cell, and—as I understand it—that is the only entrance there. There is an outside exit, but to access this, you have to go through the booking area."

***Well, all right now! The security camera is of absolutely no importance here. The security camera does not capture the incident, does not capture the cell, and only captures the hallway going to the cell. Therefore, James should be on the security camera being taken down the hallway wearing a prison uniform before midnight, then back down the hallway when he was taken out of the cell at two to use the county telephone. Then back down the hallway at 2:30. The investigating officer actually has the audacity to state, "As I understand it, that is the only entrance there." As he understands what? When I questioned him at the inquest about the other cells having showers and hidden curtain rods with no shower curtains, he distinctly told me that his investigation centered on the cell James occupied. So with such a thorough investigation of the cell James occupied, it should have been a *known* fact about the only entrance to that particular cell. Then he softly stated, "Oh, there is an outside exit, but to access this, you have to go through the booking area." Are you serious? Who better to go through the booking area to access the outside exit without any questions asked than the jail's staff? The investigating officer led the jury and my family into believing there was only one way in or out of the cell, which was not true. He kept talking about what the security camera captured. What difference did it make if nothing captured the outside exit to the cell James occupied? It is a blessing the investigating officer even mentioned the outside exit because my family was denied their request to view the cell. We would have never known there was another entrance to the cell James occupied.

The transcript stated, "At approximately 7:30 a.m., Auddie Decker, the trustee, advised that he fed breakfast to Mr. Dawson through the food port. Mr. Decker also stated that he again saw Mr. Dawson at approximately 11:05 a.m. At that time, he could see into the cell and he could see the bunk and see Mr. Dawson lying down on his bunk. He didn't know if he was asleep. Correctional Officer Deborah Cornell was the last to see him, and that was at 11:20 a.m. and she was in the kitchen area. Mrs. Cornell said she saw him lying down on his bunk." The transcript stated, "At 11:50, Deputy Cornell went to Mr. Dawson and found him partially suspended by the bed sheet tied to the shower curtain rod then again around his neck. His legs had a slight bend to them. He could have stood up, and she didn't understand this."

The transcript stated, "Do you know approximately how tall he was? I'm not sure of his height. I think approximately 5'8 – 5'9, between 222 and 240 pounds. Mrs. Dawson, the mother, said about 190. How tall was the bar in the shower? It's a little over 6'3 – 6'4, right around there. The investigating officer said, 'I weigh approximately 195 – 200 pounds, and I suspended my weight from the bar and it easily held that weight. It's done that way for a reason, for security for the jail. If a bar could easily be taken down, it could be used as a weapon. So they make these sturdy and bolt them into the wall with heavy bolts so they will not come down. It showed no signs of coming down or bending when I hung from it. It's very sturdy.'"

*** Okay, the investigating officer is certain of the sturdiness of the shower pole inside the very same cell about which he stated, "As I understand it, that is the only entrance there." The investigating officer wants to demonstrate holding onto the bar and it showing no signs of coming down or bending. I'm sure his demonstration did not consist of hanging from the bar with a bed sheet tied around his neck, choking himself to death standing on his feet. What is up with all the sturdiness in the bar, anyway? We are talking about a damn shower curtain rod with no shower curtain hanging from it! Don't you think the jail staff would be more familiar with the shower curtain rod than someone who had never been inside that cell before? It just so happened, James was chosen for that extravagant cell. I wonder if the heavily bolted shower curtain rod still exists. It's bolted so it won't be used as a weapon. What else can it be used for? As far as the investigating officer's demonstration goes, with a team of professionals willing to do everything necessary to back my theory, I think I can prove an elephant can dangle from a cliff with his tail holding onto a daisy! ***

*** Bail was paid at 11:30, just ten minutes after James was last witnessed lying down. Deputy Cornell arrived at the cell at 11:50, twenty minutes after bail was paid. So during the twenty minutes it took for Deputy Cornell to arrive at James' cell, he got up and decided to hang himself. What could have possibly happened in those twenty minutes that didn't happen in the prior nine hours? ***

The transcript stated, "Deputy Cornell commented he could have stood up, and she didn't understand this."

*** Let me try to help Deputy Cornell understand this scenario a little better. Let's say we have a 190-pound man lying down, and we have to put him in a partially hanging position. How do we determine whether he actually stood there and choked himself to death standing on his feet or was put in that position to create the appearance of a suicide—or if the hanging ever happened at all, since there are no marks on his neck?

When one thinks of a suicide hanging, one thinks of a person standing on top of an object and kicking it away. But try to visualize a person hanging with his feet resting on the floor. It is unbelievable. Studies actually show that a person does not have to be fully suspended to hang him or herself. I cannot imagine anyone being able to sustain the trauma of choking himself to death while standing. I don't care how strong a person's will is to die.

The transcript stated, "I attended the autopsy with Doctor Hindman from Springfield, and as he put in his report, I observed no trauma to Mr. Dawson whatsoever. There is a mark on his chin, underneath his chin, that was earlier at the hospital and possibly by some of the emergency medical people reported as an abrasion. At the autopsy, I asked the pathologist to explain the abrasion. He quickly corrected me and said it was not an abrasion but a pressure mark, and he said the mark occurred due to the ligature or sheet that was around Mr. Dawson's neck and had absolutely nothing to do with the death of Mr. Dawson and was not an injury, so to speak; it was caused by the sheet."

*** You mean to tell me that the investigating officer attends the autopsy, stands right there in front of the body of an alleged hanging victim, and the only thing he can tell us about is the abrasion on the chin? The family witnessed and photographed the exact same thing. In documents from the paramedics, the emergency room physician, the coroner, this investigating officer, and the Springfield pathologist, the only thing consistently reported is this mark on James' chin. None of these professionals document any marks on his neck. I realize they can only document what they observe; however, when introduced to the body of a hanging victim and the body screamed much louder than what was being presented to them, somebody should have allowed them to override what was being presented. Nobody felt able to challenge what the jail staff said happened. The investigating officer, as the one assigned to the case, should have looked for and documented marks on James' neck. Oh, that's right, the jail's staff are his friends, and he can assure the family there was no foul play involved. I almost forgot his real position. The coroner told me no one was allowed to attend the autopsy. I imagine the investigating officer was an exception to the rule. ***

When the investigating officer described the knotting of the bed sheet, he stated, "Normally we would want to preserve those knots, but when the sheriff and deputy came into the cell, their first reaction was to get him down. The sheriff told me that he thought he felt warm to the touch, and if they started CPR, they might be able to save him. The last thing on their minds was preserving the knot."

*** Yet when Mom touched James' hand as he was being put in the ambulance, his hand was "ice cold." ***

The transcript stated, "When Deputy Cornell summoned Sheriff Sowers and Deputy McCord, they came to [her] assistance and got Mr. Dawson down then started CPR. They, in turn, called the ambulance and [the paramedics] took over upon their arrival."

*** Deputy Cornell discovered the hanging at 11:50. My family sat in their vehicle for almost forty-five minutes after bail was paid at 11:30, waiting for James to be released. The Toledo ambulance arrived at the jail between 12:20 – 12:25. When was the 911 call made? That is a very long time to be in the hands of someone who must protect its facility and its staff, don't you think? You may now review the Code Blue Record:

[3171133 117:6733
DAWSON, JAMES
7/29/63 M MR :15481
EMERGENCY ROOM DOCTOR:

PRIVATE P

SARAH BUSH LINCOLN
HEALTH CENTER
1000 Health Center Drive
P.O. Box 372
Mattoon, IL 61938-0372

Type of Arrest _Cardiopulmonary_   Date _11-6-00_   Estimated Time _110 found_

Witnessed ___   Unwitnessed _X_   Site _Corr Cumberland County Jail Cell_ _1150 E ORD-_

Time CPR Started _1154_   By _Cumberland Co Sheriff et Deputy_   Initial Heart Rhythm _Ventricular fib_

Initial Skin Condition _Cyanosis under chin appl.._ Initial Pupil Response _dilated Ø reactive_

Responding Physician _Dr. Carlson/John_   Time _1237_

Intubation Time _1203_   Nasal ____   Oral _X_   ETT Size _7.5 mm 23 m/m_

Intubated by _Toledo EMT I_   Blood sugar @ scene 88

Attending Physician Notified _____ Attending Arrived _____

Consultant(s) Notified _____

Family Notified _Enroul_ #Born _____

MEDICATION LEGEND	HEART RHYTHM LEGEND	MISC. LEGEND
Epi = Epinephrine Lido = Lidocaine Atr = Atropine Iso = isoproterenol Br = Bretylium Dop = Dopamine NaHCO₃ = Sodium Bicarbonate	VF = Ventricular Fibrillation VT = Ventricular Tachycardia Asy = Asystole EMD = Electro Mechanical Dissociation AF = Atrial Fibrillation NSR = Normal Sinus Rhythm	Defib = Defibrillation Cardio = Cardioversion ETT = Endotracheal Tube EGTA = Esophageal Gastric Tube Airway ABG = Arterial Blood Gasses Ext Pac = External Pacer

Time	Blood Pressure	Pulse	Cardiac Rhythm	Medications	Defib Joules	Code Blue Notes	FR0₂
1237	—	Ø	ASY			CPR in progress Ø resp	
						effort, tachypnea respirations	
						LCA ET tube approx 2 ix	
						cyanosis noted below chin	
						Ø pulse TI IV sites Ø of (R) AC wb	
1239	—	Ø	ASY	Epi 1:10,000 IVP		CPR in progress	
1241	—					Pt log rolled maintaining	
						C-spine control Ø injury	
						Continuous cyanosis	
						noted to back	
1242	—	Ø	VF		200j	No pulseless ventricular	
						rhythm then V-FIB	
1242	—	Ø	VF		200j	remains in V-FIB	
1243	—	Ø	VF		300j	remains in V-FIB. 1000cc	
						NS infused @ T IV side repaced	
						c 1000cc N/S wide open.	
1244	—	Ø	VF		360j	remains in V-FIB	

Form No. 243
Rev 0-00

CODE BLUE RECORD

```
E        3171133  11/05/33
DAWSON, JAMES
7/29/63   M  MR    21944I
EMERGENCY ROOM DOCTORS
```

SARAH BUSH LINCOLN HEALTH CENTER
1000 Health Center Drive
P.O. Box 372
Mattoon, IL 61938-0372

Time	Blood Pressure	I/V A T Pulse	Cardiac Rhythm	Medications	Defib Joules	Code Blue Notes
1245	—	Ø	VF	Epi 1:10,000 IVP		CPR in progress.
1247	—	Ø	VF		360;	V-FIB CPR in progress, lateral C-Spine X-ray
1249	—	Ø	VF			CPR in progress
1251	—	Ø	VF	Epi 1:10,000 IVP		CPR in progress
1252	—	Ø	VF	Cordarone 300 mg IV following	360;	CPR in progress pulseless ventricular rhythm.
1257	—	Ø	ASY			H/S would of heart muscle per Dr. Ceeldotaken
1258	—	Ø	ASY	Cordarone infused		CPR in progress
1259	—	Ø	ASY	Epi 1:10000 IVP		CPR in progress
1300	—	Ø	ASY			CPR in progress
1302	—	Ø	ASY u/a vpaddles			
1303	—	Ø	ASY u/a Lead I			
1304	—	Ø	ASY u/a Lead II			
1305	—	Ø	ASY u/a Lead III			CPR efforts ceased c̄ pulse c̄ spontaneous respiratory effort pupils fixed et dilated 2250cc IV fluid infused.

Attach Strips to Separate Sheet for Documentation

Disposition of Patient CCU ___ Morgue ___ Other ___

Signature of Physicians

1 ___ 2 ___ 3 ___

Names of Persons Responding

1 ___ 5 ___ 9 ___
2 ___ 6 ___ 10 ___
3 ___ 7 ___ 11 ___
4 ___ 8 ___ 12 ___

Signature of Recorder ___

Form No. 243
Rev. 9-92

CODE BLUE RECORD

Now that we have reviewed the Code Blue record, which is documented from 12:37 until 1:05, I would like you to clearly observe:

1. Type of Arrest: Cardiopulmonary

2. Time CPR started: 11:54 by Cumberland Co. sheriff and deputy.
3. Initial skin condition: Abrasion under the chin, 2 inch in length.
4. Responding Physician: Dr. Czelatdko Time 12:37
5. Intubation time 12:03   Intubated by Toledo Emergency Medical Team
6. At 12:37, the Code Blue notes: "CPR in progress, no respirations effort, bagging respirations via ET tube approx. 2 in abrasion noted below the chin right side."
7. At 12:41, the Code Blue notes: "Pt log rolled maintaining C-spine control. No injury contusions/abrasions noted to back."
8. At 12:53, the Code Blue notes: "CPR in progress pulseless ventricular rhythm u/s visual of heart muscle per Dr. Czelatdko."

3, 6, and 7 are the only documentation of marks noted on the Code Blue record.

#4. The responding physician, Dr. Czelatdko, is the emergency room physician at Sarah Bush Lincoln Health Center. He is the one who informed the family that James was dead. How can his response time be 12:37, the same time the family witnessed the ambulance leaving the jail? Remember, the family waited in their vehicle for almost forty-five minutes after bail was paid at 11:30, until around 12:15. Shortly after that, the clerk came to their vehicle to inform them of a medical emergency. Shortly after that, the Toledo ambulance arrived at the jail, at around 12:20 – 12:25. Shortly after that, James was being carried out of the jail into the ambulance, at around 12:35 – 12:40. The family followed the Toledo ambulance for about twenty minutes to Sarah Bush Lincoln Health Center, for a distance of 19.46 miles. Keep in mind, the ambulance stopped for a few minutes while one of the paramedics conversed with another before reaching the hospital. James was dead on arrival and pronounced dead at 1:05. So again, how can the emergency room physician, who was not at the jail, have responded at 12:37?

#5. How can the Toledo emergency medical team have intubated James at 12:03 when they did not arrive at the jail until 12:20 – 12:25? Supposedly, the jail staff started CPR at 11:54. Since the intubation time is recorded at 12:03 and James was said to have been intubated by the Toledo emergency medical team inside the jail, it is nine minutes after the jail staff started their CPR. I realize the ambulance department is located in the same area as the jail, so how did this particular emergency team get inside James' cell? Did they perhaps go through the mysterious outside exit that can only be accessed by going through the booking area? They definitely did not arrive with the ambulance.

#8. The Code Blue started at 12:37, the same time as the family witnessed the ambulance leaving the jail and continued until 1:05, when James was pronounced dead. Throughout the Code Blue record, they did not mention the emergency room physician Dr. Czelatdko until 12:53. From 12:53 until 1:05 after Dr Czelatdko pronounced James dead is the 10 minute period my family recalls his actions. You may now review the Emergency Room Record:

SARAH BUSH LINCOLN HEALTH CENTER
1000 HEALTH CENTER DRIVE
MATTOON, IL 61938

EMERGENCY ROOM RECORD

DATE: 11/06/2000

CHIEF COMPLAINT: This is a 37-year-old black male who presents to the emergency department from jail with apparent hanging injury.

HISTORY OF PRESENT ILLNESS: The paramedics report that the patient was found hanging with possibly a sheet in his cell and was taken down by jail staff before they arrived. They report that the patient was last seen at that evaluation although the paramedics report that inmate evaluations were at least thirty minutes apart. There was no prior report of the patient reporting suicidal ideation, chest pain, shortness of breath, or any other complaint.

PAST MEDICAL HISTORY: Denies.

MEDICATIONS: None per the family.

ALLERGIES: NONE PER THE FAMILY.

SOCIAL HISTORY: The patient was in jail for being caught while driving under suspended license.

EMERGENCY ROOM COURSE: The patient was evaluated at the scene and intercept was called for. The patient was rapidly transported to the hospital and intubated in the field with good breath sounds bilateral. The patient had an IV started as well and advanced cardiac life support protocol was initiated at the scene. The patient arrived unresponsive, no pulse, no spontaneous respirations. The patient was intubated with equal breath sounds. The patient had aggressive advanced cardiac life support protocol although these were unsuccessful. The patient was pronounced dead at 1305 and had no signs of life, no spontaneous respirations, and asystole on the monitor in more than two leads. The coroner was notified and the case was discussed at length with the family. The case was also discussed with the sheriff's office.

DIAGNOSES:
1.   CARDIOPULMONARY ARREST.
2.   POSSIBLE ASPHYXIATION SECONDARY TO HANGING INJURY PER HISTORY.

End of document.

Signed: _____
        Thomas Czelatdko, D.O.

DAWSON, JAMES
3171130   (000219481)
Patient Type: E/O
Admit Date: 11/06/2000
jas   Date Dictated: 11/06/2000

Location: E 0000
    Date of Birth: 07/29/1963

Previous Location:

Date Transcribed: 11/07/2000

The emergency room course stated The patient arrived unresponsive, no pulse, no spontaneous respirations. James was not declared dead at the hospital. D.O.A. has been documented on the death certificate. The last I checked, D.O.A. meant dead on arrival and not dead after arrival. You may now review the death certificate:

There were several correspondences between Sarah Bush Lincoln Health Center and me after I requested and received a copy of James' medical records. After receiving the emergency room physician's bill for $648 for direct advanced life and heart/lung resuscitation performed at the Sarah Bush Lincoln Health Center's emergency room, we later received another bill for $1,958.50, for a total of $2,606.50.

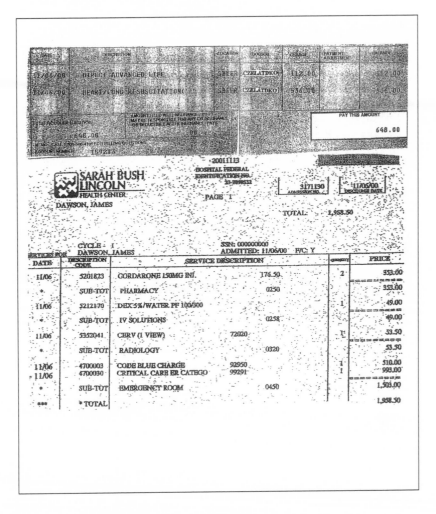

I wrote a letter to Dr. Czelatdko questioning him about his bill. I also questioned the critical care emergency room catego in the amount of $993 because I could not understand how we could receive a bill from the emergency room physician and the emergency room. Here is the letter sent to Dr. Czelatdko, followed by the response received from the risk manager:

Dr. Thomas Czelatdko
c/o Sarah Bush Lincoln Health Center
1000 Health Center Drive
P.O. Box 372
Mattoon Ill. 61938 – 0372

To Dr. Czelatdko:

We, the family of James Dawson have received your medical bill totaling $648. On November 6, 2000, we arrived at Sarah Bush Lincoln Health Center along with the Toledo ambulance. We watched you attending to James for about ten minutes before you came to inform us that he was dead. According to your emergency room report, you stated, "The patient arrived unresponsive, no pulse, no spontaneous respirations." According to the Code Blue report, no pulse was documented from 12:37 until 1:05. According to the death certificate, D.O.A was documented. Since there was no pulse for twenty-eight minutes, and James' hand was "ice cold" when his mother touched him as he was being placed inside the ambulance, and although you pronounced him dead at 1:05, the question is what time did James really die?

Since James arrived at Sarah Bush Lincoln Health Center unresponsive, with no pulse, no spontaneous respirations, you still provided aggressive advanced cardiac life support protocol, although this was unsuccessful. This is where your bill for direct advanced life and heart/lung resuscitation comes in. In addition to your bill, we received a separate bill from your hospital for $1,958.50. Is this the paramedics bill? I noticed there is a charge for $993.00 for critical care emergency room catageo, what is that for? More importantly, while viewing James' body after you pronounced him dead, the family witnessed no marks on his neck. We tried to locate you, but we were told that you were not available. However, we did locate the recording nurse and escorted her back to the room where James' body lay and questioned her about why were there no marks on his neck if he died from hanging. Of course, she could not explain this. Unfortunately, you and the recording nurse gave two different objects that had supposedly surrounded the neck. Nevertheless, there should have been some kind of ligature mark on the neck, regardless of what had supposedly surrounded it. So Dr. Czelatdko, what marks did you personally witness on the neck of this alleged hanging victim? There is no documentation of any marks on your report.

We notice in your chief complaint you stated, "James was presented to the emergency department with apparent hanging injury." Your diagnoses stated, "Possible asphyxiation secondary to hanging injury per history." What does this mean? We realize you can only go with what has been presented to you by the paramedics and the jail staff, however the question remains, what marks did you witness on the neck? Any answers you are able to provide would be greatly appreciated.

SARAH BUSH LINCOLN
HEALTH CENTER

Dear Ms. Dawson:

This letter is in follow up to a letter recently received by one of our Emergency Department Physicians, Dr. Thomas Czelatdko. The letter requested information regarding the care and treatment rendered to your son surrounding his death on 11/6/00. As the Risk Manager for Sarah Bush Lincoln, which employs Dr. Czelatdko, I am responding to your letter on his behalf.

I regret to inform you that we are unable to provide further insight into the circumstances surrounding the events leading up to your sons presentation at our Emergency department. I believe our Patient Representative Ms. Peggy Clark, has provide you with whatever information we have access to. I understand your concern and dedication to finding out further information concerning your sons death, however, due to the fact that our staff was not present at the Cumberland County Jail we just do not have the answers you are looking for. My suggestion is that you retain the services of an attorney or private detective who would be better able to access the information you are requesting.

In addition, in response to your questions regarding the bill from Sarah Bush Lincoln with respect to the $993.00 for the Critical Care ED charge, they are customary charges for nursing and other ancillary care provided during the period of time your son was being attended to in our Emergency Department. There was period of 28 minutes when a team of medical professionals were diligently attempting to resuscitate your son. Those charges are for their services. In addition there were charges for medication and a code blue charge for the necessary emergency supplies. I hope this answers any questions you may have regarding the charges.

Once again, our condolences on your sons death. We wish you the best in your quest to uncover the facts and circumstances surrounding his death.

Sincerely,

Cheryl M Creasy RN, MBA
Cheryl M Creasy, RN, MBA
Director, Case/Quality/Risk Management

First, we appreciate the risk manager's suggestion that we retain the services of an attorney or private detective who would be better able to access the information we requested, but she gave us all the information we needed. She stated, "Our staff was not present at the jail." Therefore, Dr. Czelatdko was not at the jail. She stated that the $993 for critical care emergency room charge were customary charges for nursing and other ancillary care provided during the time James was being attended to in their emergency room department. There were twenty-eight minutes during which a team of medical professionals diligently attempted to resuscitate him, and those charges were for their services.

I thoroughly re-examined the risk manager's statement which according to the patient registration form James was admitted inside Sarah Bush Lincoln Health Center at 12:31. Here is a copy of the admittance time:

The admittance time (12:31) will validate the emergency medical team being inside the jail at 12:03, which is when the intubation was said to have been performed by them. Transporting James to Sarah Bush Lincoln Health Center, life support was administered in route. Again the distance from the jail to the hospital is 19.46 miles an estimated time of twenty eight minutes. So from 12:03, the intubation time until 12:31 the admittance time, is twenty eight minutes. I assumed that was the twenty eight minutes the risk manager was referring to. Not so fast!

The emergency room physician response time is at 12:37 which is six minutes after James arrived inside the hospital dead on arrival at 12:31. The physician performed advanced cardiac life support from 12:37 until 1:05. That is also twenty eight minutes. My question is, what happened from 12:31 until 12:37? Is it medically possible to resuscitate someone six minutes after arriving dead on arrival? If so, for twenty eight minute?

There is always two sides to a story and my family's recollection of what happened is completely different. My family clearly recalled paying bail at 11:30 and being sent back to their vehicle to wait on James to be released. They clearly recalled looking at the clock watching the time past for almost forty five minutes before the clerk came to inform them of a medical emergency which was the delay in James release. They clearly recalled watching the ambulance arrive between 12:20 and 12:25. They clearly recalled watching James being carried out of the jail into the ambulance wearing his underwear and socks. They clearly recalled running to the ambulance and mom touching James hand which was cold as ice. They clearly recalled following the ambulance from 12:35 for about twenty minutes to the hospital. They clearly recalled watching the emergency physician work on James for about ten minutes before he came to inform them of his death.

So what the risk manager wants us to believe is that the paramedics worked on James in route to the hospital for twenty eight minutes then once he arrived at the hospital dead on arrival, six minutes later, the hospital staff worked on him for an additional twenty eight minutes. Please, let us reiterate the emergency room course once again. It stated "the patient was evaluated at the scene and intercept was called for. The patient was rapidly transported to the hospital and intubated in the field with good breath sounds bilateral. The patient had IV started as well and advanced cardiac life support protocol was initiated at the scene. The patient arrived unresponsive with no pulse and no spontaneous respirations." That was the end of the performances done by the paramedics. The emergency room physician took over from there. "The patient was intubated with equal breath sounds. The patient had aggressive advanced cardiac life support protocol although unsuccessful." That was the end of the performances done by the emergency room physician and the hospital staff. James was pronounced dead at 1305 and had no signs of life, and no spontaneous respirations.

Nevertheless, I had assumed the activities recorded on the code blue report were from the paramedics since my family recalled following them at 12:37 to the hospital before James was pronounced dead at 1:05. However, according to the admittance time the paramedics performances were completed at 12:31. Therefore, the activities recorded on the code blue report are from the emergency physician and the hospital staff and not the paramedics. Let us move on to the emergency room report. It stated

Chief complaint: "This is a 37-year-old black male who presents to the emergency department from jail with apparent hanging injury."

Apparent means: "Readily seen, visible, readily understood or perceived; evident, obvious, appearing (but not necessarily) real or true, seeming."

History of present illness: "The paramedics report that the patient was found hanging with possibly a sheet in his cell and was taken down by the jail staff before they arrived."

Diagnoses: Cardiopulmonary Arrest. Possible asphyxiation secondary to hanging injury per history.

Whenever I heard the words "possibly" or "possible," it means it could go either way. It could mean it happened just as strongly as it could mean it might not have happened. It's not a sure thing! Injury per history is what the jail staff said happened.

Cardiopulmonary arrest means the heart (cardio) and lungs (pulmonary) stopped working. The heart expands and contacts under the control of a special group of pace-making cells. The pump action of the heart pushes blood teeming with oxygen and other nutrients out to the rest of the body. If the heart is not beating properly, or at all, blood is not supplied to the body, and oxygen and other vital nutrients are not delivered to the tissues and organs (including the heart.) With no energy to power the body, vital organs like the heart and lungs stop working, and you are left in a state of cardiopulmonary arrest.

Cardiopulmonary arrest is extremely dangerous. Within four to six minutes without oxygen, brain cells begin to die off rapidly. With each additional minute, the damage builds up; most people cannot survive long in this state.

According to my family, it took the ambulance at least thirty to thirty-five minutes to arrive at the jail after James was said to have been found hanging. I wrote a letter to the Toledo ambulance department and mailed it twice, but they did not respond. Here is the letter:

Toledo Ambulance Department
P.O. Box 516
Toledo, Ill. 62468

RE: Questions regarding procedures taken by your emergency medical team on November 6, 2000 inside and outside the Cumberland County jail.

To whom it may concern:

A 911 call was made about a hanging discovered at 11:50 a.m. by the Cumberland County jail staff. The family of James Dawson was sitting in their vehicle waiting on him to be released after they paid bail. The family clearly recalls the Toledo ambulance arriving at the jail around 12:20 – 12:25. The family followed the Toledo ambulance to Sarah Bush Lincoln Health Center. The questions are what time was the 911 call received by your establishment? What time according to your records did your crew arrive at the jail?

According to official documents, when your crew arrived at the jail, James was lying on the floor, and CPR was in progress. When your crew arrived, what clothes did James have on his body? I pose this question because the family witnessed James being carried out of the jail only wearing his underwear and socks. I can understand why the prison shirt would have to be removed to try to revive an alleged hanging victim, but I cannot understand why the prison pants had to be removed.

While following your crew to the hospital for about twenty minutes, the family witnessed them stop to converse with another ambulance waiting with its lights flashing. Is it protocol for your crew to stop to converse with another during an emergency before reaching the hospital? Any answers you are able to provide would be greatly appreciated.

When I received no response from the Toledo Ambulance Department, of course, I was not surprised. I mean, come on now; they are neighbors to the jail. When we start talking about "to serve and to protect," that is exactly what they are going to do for one another.

Anyway, still baffled about why James was brought out of the jail only wearing his underwear and socks, I wrote a letter to Sarah Bush Lincoln Health Center about the emergency department record-nursing document I found in James' medical records. It was difficult to read so I had them to transcribe it for me. That transcript reads, "Found hanging in jail cell, down time at least thirty minutes. Code Blue report from Cumberland County Jail. Bond had been posted and patient was released then found hanging. Ambulance state crew found body on the floor CPR in progress by correctional officers. 12:50 G. Rollins, State Police District #10 notified. See Code Blue Sheet, 13:07 Officer Maroon, Cumberland County Sheriff's department here. 13:15 clothing of patient in paper bags. 1 gray and white-striped shirt, 1 pair white socks, 1 white Bulls t-shirt, 1 Hanes jockey shorts, 1 gray and white-striped jail pants given to Officer Maroon. See Code Blue Summary. 13:28 Coroner Mike Nichols here, tubes pulled, family in room. 14:55 body transported to Springfield.

I read at 12:50 "G. Rollins, State Police District #10 was initially notified"; what happened to him? They went completely out of their district to state police headquarters District #9, to assign the case to Mr. Kelly Hodge, who could assure the family there was no foul play involved because the jail people were his friends. Then they notified G. Rollins fifteen minutes before James was pronounced dead.

Also it stated, "Code Blue report from Cumberland County jail." Not Code Blue report from Sarah Bush Lincoln Health Center. Why would the report be from the jail when according to the admittance form, James was in the hospital at 12:31? Here is the emergency department record-nursing document:

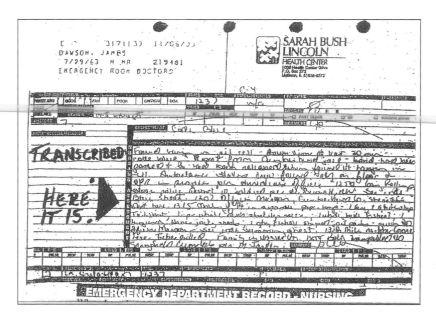

When I read at 13:07 Officer Maroon, Cumberland County Sheriff's department arrived, I thought, he really didn't waste any time getting there, did he? James was pronounced dead at 13:05. Then when I read that at 13:15, the clothing of the patient was given to Officer Maroon in paper bags, I was like wow! We'd been looking for these clothes. Who gave Officer Maroon the clothes? Did the paramedics take clothes not on James' body and leave them for Officer Maroon? How did the clothes arrive at the hospital? At least it stated they were given to Officer Maroon in paper bags, meaning there was more than one bag. I still can not understand why the clothes were given to Officer Maroon in the first place. When the family went to the room to view James' body, he was naked and covered with a white sheet; therefore, the white socks and Hanes jockey shorts were removed in the emergency room at the hospital. I wonder what happened to the clothes that were given to Officer Maroon. Here is the response from Sarah Bush Lincoln Health Center:

Peggy Clark, R.N.
Patient Representative
1000 Health Center Drive
Mattoon, IL 61938
217-258/348-2491

Dear Ms. Dawson:

I am in receipt of your letter post-marked March 2, 2001. Unfortunately, I do not have the answers to your questions. My resource is the medical record, which you also have and I only know what is documented there.

The nurse who documented on the emergency room record no longer works at Sarah Bush Lincoln Health Center, so it is not possible for me to contact her to clarify answers for you.

I believe Sheriff Steve Maroon or the EMT team who responded could better answer the questions you have posed. My suggestion is that you contact either or both of them.

Sincerely,

Peggy Clark RN

Peggy Clark, R.N.
Patient Representative

PC/caw

1000 Health Center Drive • P.O. Box 372 • Mattoon, IL 61938-0372 • 217-258-2525 (Mattoon) • 217-348-2525 (Charleston) • 217-258-2288 (FAX)

I tried contacting Sheriff Maroon and the ambulance department, but got no response. When I read that the nurse who signed off on the emergency room record no longer worked at the hospital, I couldn't help but wonder if it was the same nurse Michael had taken to the room and asked why there were no marks on James' neck. Well, I couldn't help but wonder.

I wrote a letter to the Memorial Medical Center in Springfield, where Mr. Travis Hindman performed the autopsy and got rid of all internal organs, tissues, brain, and blood without notifying the family and without authorization from the family. I sent the letter twice by certified mail with the return receipt requested to verify that my letters were received. However, Memorial Medical Center did not respond. Here is the proof of delivery, followed by the letter:

received February 19, 2002

SENDER: *COMPLETE THIS SECTION*	COMPLETE THIS SECTION ON DELIVERY
■ Complete items 1, 2, and 3. Also complete Item 4 if Restricted Delivery is desired. ■ Print your name and address on the reverse so that we can return the card to you. ■ Attach this card to the back of the mailpiece, or on the front if space permits.	A. Signature Memorial Medical Center X ☐ Agent ☐ Addressee B. Received by (*Printed Name*) C. Date of Delivery
1. Article Addressed to: *MEMORIAL MEDICAL CENTER* *701 N. FIRST STREET* *Springfield, Ill.* *62781*	D. Is delivery address different from item 1? ☐ Yes If YES, enter delivery address below: ☐ No 3. Service Type ☐ Certified Mail ☐ Express Mail ☐ Registered ☐ Return Receipt for Merchandise ☐ Insured Mail ☐ C.O.D. 4. Restricted Delivery? (*Extra Fee*) ☐ Yes
2. Article Number (*Transfer from service label*) *7001-1940-0005-8979-0010*	
PS Form 3811, August 2001 Domestic Return Receipt 102595-01-M-0361	

received March 11, 2002

SENDER: *COMPLETE THIS SECTION*	COMPLETE THIS SECTION ON DELIVERY
■ Complete items 1, 2, and 3. Also complete Item 4 if Restricted Delivery is desired. ■ Print your name and address on the reverse so that we can return the card to you. ■ Attach this card to the back of the mailpiece, or on the front if space permits.	A. Signature X ☐ Agent ☐ Addressee B. Received by (*Printed Name*) C. Date of Delivery
1. Article Addressed to: *MEMORIAL MEDICAL CENTER* *701 N. FIRST STREET* *Springfield, Ill* *62781*	D. Is delivery address different from item 1? ☐ Yes If YES, enter delivery address below: ☐ No 3. Service Type ☐ Certified Mail ☐ Express Mail ☐ Registered ☐ Return Receipt for Merchandise ☐ Insured Mail ☐ C.O.D. 4. Restricted Delivery? (*Extra Fee*) ☐ Yes
2. Article Number (*Transfer from service label*) 7001 1940 0005 8974 8427	
PS Form 3811, August 2001 Domestic Return Receipt 102595-01-M-2509	

Memorial Medical Center
701 First Street
Springfield Ill. 62781

RE: Actions regarding an autopsy performed at your establishment.

To the chief of staff or whomever it may concern:

I, Margaret (Dawson)   Brown am writing in regards

to an autopsy performed at your establishment on November 7, 2000, at approximately 8:30 a.m. The patient James Dawson, autopsy #CC-328-00. The autopsy was performed by Mr. Travis Hindman. I have received a copy of the autopsy report, which lists seventeen categories to represent the examination performed to determine the cause of death from a hanging victim. Unfortunately, there is no mention of any marks on the neck of this alleged hanging victim. I realize your pathologist could only document what he observed, however, the family of James Dawson was able to witness and photograph the body immediately after he was pronounced dead, and there are no marks on his neck. I know it should be protocol for your establishment to also photograph the neck of a hanging victim, so my question is, do you have those photographs on file?

The internal examination performed by your pathologist consisted of getting rid of all internal organs, all tissues, including the brain, and doing a complete blood drainage. Is this the normal procedure at your establishment? If so, how can a procedure of this nature take place without notifications to families and without authorizations from families? What happened to all of James Dawson's organs? Had the family not requested an independent re-autopsy, we would have never known everything was completely cleaned out by your pathologist. Any information you are able to provide would be greatly appreciated.

Destroyed about the missing organs, I am still looking for answers. I noticed in James' medical records there is a "death summary" document, in which a "suitable donor" decision had been checked off. The name of transplant coordinator was Brendan Glynn #0040373 @13:45, forty minutes after James was pronounced dead. I contacted Sarah Bush Lincoln Health Center about the suitable donor decision, and here is what they had to say:

**SARAH BUSH
LINCOLN**
HEALTH CENTER

February 27, 2001

Dear Mrs. Dawson:

I am responding to the letter which you sent to Tina Butler. May I first express sincere sympathy to you in the loss of your son.

I have researched answers to your questions by speaking with medical records, reviewing James' record, conversing with ROBI and the Director of the Emergency Department.

There was no harvest of any organs from your son. This information is supported by a supervisor at ROBI. The absence of other required documentation from James' chart supports this also.

I am unable to explain why the Death Summary indicates the information it does and unfortunately the nurse who signed the sheet has moved on to another position away from our area.

If you have more questions I would be happy to assist you as would Sue at ROBI.

Sincerely,

Peggy Clark, R.N.
Patient Representative

Here is the death summary document followed by the autopsy report from Springfield:

[3171133 117??713]		
DAWSON, JAMES		
7/29/63 · M MR 27-4HT		

SARAH BUSH LINCOLN
HEALTH CENTER
1000 Health Center Drive
P.O. Box 372
Mattoon, IL 61938-0372

Addressograph

A. Death occurred on ___11-6-00___ at ___1805___
    (date)   (time)

B. Tissue Donation
  1. Notify ROBI on all deaths (telephone # 1-800-545-4438)
  2. Name of transplant coordinator contacted: ___Brendan Glynn___ #0040373@1345
    (Name)
  3. Decision of transplant coordinator:
    ☑ Suitable donor
    ☐ Not suitable donor
      If not, reason:
  4. Family approached by: ☑ ROBI ☐ SBLHC requestor
    ☐ Agrees
      ☐ Consent completed
    ☐ Disagrees - complete following with family:
      ☐ I have been offered the opportunity to allow a tissue donation. I have refused this opportunity.

_____   _____   _____
(Signature)   (Relationship to patient)   (Date/Time)
  5. Family not approached because:
    ☐ The existence of the person is unknown to the Health Center personnel, and is not readily ascertainable through the examination of the decedent's hospital records and the questioning of any persons who are available for giving consent.
    OR
    ☐ Health Center personnel have been unsuccessful in attempting to contact the person by telephone or any other reasonable manner.

C. Physician(s) Notified
  Name_____ Date_____ Time_____
  Name_____ Date_____ Time_____
  Name_____ Date_____ Time_____

D. Family Notified ☑ Family Present)
  Name _Lila Dawson_____ Date_____ Time_____
  Name_____ Date_____ Time_____

E. Coroner Notified ☑ Yes ☐ No   Date _11-6-00_ Time _1315_ ☐ N/A
                              her @ 1508
  Funeral Home Notified: Date_____ Time_____ Name_____
  Address_____
  Pt. had infectious disease prior to death ☐ Yes ☐ No
  If Yes, funeral home advised and body labeled ☐ Yes ☐ No   _Jo Williams_ RN

Release Signatures   ☑ Personal Belongings Received
Nearest Relative/Health Care POA: _Lillie Dawson_ Relationship: _mother_
Funeral Home _A R Leak_ _Walter Bruce_ Date _11/6/00_ Time _255 PM_
Hospital Personnel _____ Date _11-6-00_ Time _1403_

DEATH SUMMARY

TRAVIS L. HINDMAN, MD
FORENSIC MEDICAL SERVICES
SPRINGFIELD, ILLINOIS

AUTOPSY NUMBER
CC-328-00

CORONER
MICHAEL NICHOLS

COUNTY OF JURISDICTION
COLES

NAME : JAMES DAWSON **SEX:** Female **AGE:** 37 **DOB:** 7/29/63 **RACE:** Black
RESIDENCE: Chicago, IL

OFFICIAL DATE/TIME OF DEATH: 11/6/00 at 1305 hrs
PLACE OF DEATH: Sarah Bush Lincoln Health Center, Mattoon, IL
DATE OF REPORT: 11/17/2000
DATE OF AUTOPSY: 11/7/00 at 0830 hrs
REPORT PREPARED BY: Travis L. Hindman, MD.
AUTOPSY PERFORMED AT: Memorial Medical Center, Springfield, IL

FINAL AUTOPSY DATA SUMMARY
(Based upon all information and findings available on the date of this report)

1. Historical information typical of partial suspension hanging by the neck

2. Severe bilateral pulmonary congestion and edema

3. Pressure mark beneath the chin secondary to the presence of the bed sheet ligature surrounding the neck

4. No evidence of atherosclerosis of the coronary arteries or aorta

5. Tunneling (bridging) of the anterior descending branch of the left coronary artery

6. No evidence of recent trauma

7. No evidence of significant pathologic processes

8. Blood ethanol: no detectable level
9. Urine ethanol: no detectable level
10. Vitreous ethanol: no detectable level
    - by head space gas chromatography

11. Carboxyhemoglobin concentration: <1.0% hemoglobin saturation by cooximeter

12. Blood drug screen: no detectable level of drugs identified by enzyme immunoassay, thin layer and gas chromatography

13. Urine drug screen: no detectable level of drugs identified by enzyme immunoassay and thin layer chromatography

14. Cyanide screen: negative by colorimetric spot test

15. Right and left nasal swabs: no detectable level of cocaine identified by gas chromatography

16. Blood group and type: B positive

17. Antibodies to Human Immunodeficiency Virus: non reactive

AUTOPSY SUMMARY

Information regarding the circumstances of death is obtained from: Coles County Coroner, Michael Nichols, Kelly Hodge Illinois State Police and Steve Maroon, Cumberland County Sheriff's Department (Chief Deputy Sheriff) and from the medical records of Sarah Bush Lincoln Health Center, Mattoon, IL.

The decedent is a 37-year-old black gentleman who was temporarily incarcerated at the Cumberland County jail in Toledo, IL on 11/6/00. The decedent was arrested for speeding and was driving with a suspended driver's license. This lead to his being jailed. It was also known that the decedent's wife had left him. The decedent was in his cell alone and when the attendants went to the jail cell he was hanging by the neck with a bed sheet tied to a shower curtain rod on the inside of the shower stall. The exact knotting method around the neck is not known at the time of this writing. The body was taken down and transported via ambulance to Sarah Bush Lincoln Health Center, Mattoon, IL where he was pronounced dead after resuscitative efforts failed to revive him. The decedent was thought to have a small abrasion underneath his chin, which was secondary to the bed sheet. The decedent's habits regarding the use of drugs and alcohol are not known at the time of this writing. The decedent's medical history is not known at the time of this writing. The decedent had been incarcerated in the Cumberland County jail for approximately 12 hours. He was last seen alive at 1120 hours on 11/6/00. The body was discovered at 1150 hours. White clear saliva was noted coming from the mouth at the time of discovery. The decedent was partially suspended with his feet resting on the floor and with a slight bend in one knee.

The major findings and conclusions based upon the known circumstances of death, microscopic examination and additional testing are as follows:

A mark beneath the chin was secondary to the pressure of the bed sheet surrounding the neck during a partial suspension hanging. No other forms of trauma were identified. There was no evidence of significant disease process. There was tunneling (bridging) of the anterior descending branch of the left coronary artery, a congenital anomaly. This did not contribute to death. The post mortem body fluids toxicology was negative.

11/17/2000

Travis L. Hindman, MD

Report of Coroner's Physician to the

Coroner of _____ COLES _____ County, Illinois

I, _____ Travis L Hindman _____ M. D., have examined have made a necropsy on the

body identified to me by the coroner of this county as being:

Name ____ James Dawson ____ Date of Death 11/6/00 ____

Place of Death (city, village, or twp.) _____ Mattoon, Illinois _____

Place of Examination (city, village, or twp.) _____ Springfield, Illinois _____

In my opinion, the cause of death was as follows:

[Enter only one cause per line for (a), (b), and (c).]

IMMEDIATE CAUSE

(a) Hanging by the neck, partial suspension

DUE TO, OR AS A CONSEQUENCE OF

(b)

DUE TO, OR AS A CONSEQUENCE OF:

(c)

CONDITIONS, IF ANY, WHICH GAVE RISE TO IMMEDIATE CAUSE (a) STATING THE UNDERLYING CAUSE LAST.

OTHER SIGNIFICANT CONDITIONS CONTRIBUTING TO DEATH BUT NOT RELATED TO THE TERMINAL CONDITIONS GIVEN ABOVE.

None

My conclusions are based on the following observations and findings.

My conclusions are based upon the known circumstances of death as related to me at the time of autopsy, the postmortem examination, and various laboratory studies.

A mark beneath the chin was secondary to the pressure of the bed sheet surrounding the neck during a partial suspension hanging. No other forms of trauma were identified. There was no evidence of significant disease process. There was tunneling (bridging) of the anterior descending branch of the left coronary artery, a congenital anomaly. This did not contribute to death. The post mortem body fluids toxicology was negative.

Date ____ 11/17/2000 ____ Signed _____ M. D.

Coroner's Physician

INSTRUCTIONS: 1. Prepare this form in triplicate. Use typewriter for all entries except signature.
2. Sign original and first copy in pen and ink.

First, the autopsy states that James is female; he was a male. There were seventeen categories listed, and believe it or not, none of them document any marks on James' neck. They almost got me when I read #3.) "Pressure mark beneath the chin, secondary to the presence of the bed sheet ligature surrounding the neck." You see, a "ligature" is what I am looking for. I am looking for somebody, anybody, to document a ligature mark on James' neck to verify that a hanging actually took place. Only the pathologist used the word ligature to describe the bed sheet. Let's rewind to the investigating officer's testimony, to when he questioned the pathologist about the mark on James' chin: "The mark was not an abrasion but a pressure mark, and the mark occurred due to the ligature or sheet that was around Mr. Dawson's neck."

Why isn't anybody talking about the marks the bed sheet made on his neck? With all of this attention brought to a mark on James' chin, and nothing mentioned about the marks on his neck, it automatically raises a red flag. None of these individuals can document or elaborate on something that's just not there. Looking at the seventeen categories listed, none appears to necessitate the removal of all organs, tissues, or blood drainage. It startled me when I read in the pathologist's summary, "It was known that the decedent's wife had left him." What is that all about? I realize they needed ammunition to bring their suicide story to life, but that one is not going to work. James' wife did not leave him. James and his wife were separated, and he had moved back home with our parents. Mom had disclosed this information to the investigating officer when he questioned her at the jail. Even when they state they took James to the booking area to use the county phone after he tried to make a collect call from his cell at two in the morning, they asked if he was married and he said, "Yeah, on paper." I cannot see his marital status coming up at that moment. When James was being processed, James had plenty of pictures of him and his wife, so I can see his marital status coming up then. I personally think the pathologist needed to concentrate on the facts before him, like documenting marks on James' neck.

The autopsy summary stated, "White, clear saliva was noted coming from James' mouth at the time of discovery." It's strange the pathologist would even mention this because Michael also noticed white foam coming from James' mouth as he was being carried into the ambulance. I told Michael the white foam was probably from the tubes in James' mouth, but Michael tried to convince me, and anybody who would listen to him, that his uncle was poisoned. That is why one of the letters addressed to Mom stated that the second autopsy indicated poison; however, that was Michael's theory. Strangely, Leak's staff informed me that white fluid was noted coming from his penis. That is an area I really do not want to go into, especially since James was brought out of the jail only wearing his underwear and socks and his cell had a back entrance.

Going back to the proceedings, the record stated that the officer who stopped James for speeding and arrested him had asked him where he was going. James said he was just out driving. He said he didn't have a destination in mind. The officer said James was nervous, but that is not uncommon for someone being stopped by a police officer. The officer said James said he needed to talk with somebody, and the officer asked what he meant. He asked if James was talking about a counselor. James said, "No, you will do," and then told the officer that he and his wife were separated.

*** This is where I thought we had entered the wrong proceedings because James would have never just started talking to anybody, especially a stranger and a traffic cop, about his personal business like that. That was not his M.O. The separation had happened over six months before, and James and his wife had already moved on with their lives. I don't care how nervous he was; that conversation would have never come up. Why wouldn't he have started talking about the court date for the following day, for what the officer was citing him for—speeding and a suspended license? He was not cited for no proof of insurance, even though the suspension was an SR-22 insurance suspension. He was headed back home so he wouldn't miss his court date. Why wouldn't that conversation have come into play instead of a separation that happened over six months before? It's amazing how the investigating officer's questions to Mom were the ammunition they tried to use to build their case. Although the investigating officer did talk to James' wife to confirm the separation, she gave him no details, so he was unaware it had happened over six months before. They tried to use the separation as if it had just happened. By the way, where is the arresting officer, because according to the Office of the Secretary of State and James' driver's record, there was no citation issued to him on the night of November 5, 2000.***

The coroner tops off his autopsy summary by stating that the decedent's habits regarding the use of drugs or alcohol were not known at the time of his writing. Yet according to the tests he performed, the blood and urine screen showed no detectable level of drugs. What is the Springfield pathologist looking for or trying to insinuate? Here is my research on how autopsies are usually performed:

What happens after death? > Autopsies >

What is an autopsy?

An autopsy, also called a post-mortem examination, is a detailed and careful medical examination of a person's body and its organs after death to help establish the cause of death. The word autopsy is derived from a Greek word *autopsia* meaning 'seeing for oneself'. A physician, called a pathologist, who specialises in the study of human diseases, performs the autopsy. Surgical techniques are used to remove and examine each organ, and some tissue samples are selected for microscopic examination or other special tests as required. (A small tissue sample is typically about 0.5cm thick).

An autopsy is usually carried out within 48 hours after the death of a person. An autopsy can be hospital-based (non-coronial) or coronial. Coronial autopsies are ordered by the state coroner, whereas hospital based autopsies may be performed at the request of the family of the deceased.

There are three levels of autopsy

1. Complete - in which all body cavities are examined (including the head)
2. Limited - which may exclude the head
3. Selective- where specific organs only are examined.

Autopsies will usually include testing for any infections (microbiology), changes in body tissue and organs (anatomical histology), and chemicals, eg medication, drugs or poisons (toxicology and pharmacology).

In certain circumstances an autopsy might not be carried out if the coroner and a forensic pathologist can decide the cause of death from medical history and a police report.

What happens after death? > Autopsies >

Steps of an autopsy

1. The pathologist records the results of the external examination and lists all physical characteristics. The body must be measured and weighed and placed on an autopsy table. An autopsy table is waist-high stainless steel with running to facilitate washing away all the blood that is released during the procedure. The autopsy table is a slanted tray (for drainage) with raised edges (to keep blood and fluids from flowing onto the floor).

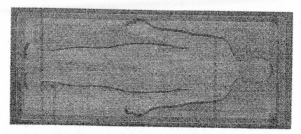

2. The first cut known as the 'Y' incision is made. The arms of the Y extend from the front of each shoulder to the bottom end of the breastbone. The tail of the Y extends from the sternum to the pubic bone and typically deviates to avoid the navel. The incision is very deep, extending to the rib cage on the chest; and completely through the abdominal wall below that. The skin from this cut is peeled back, with the top flap pulled over the face.

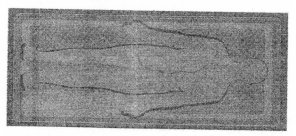

3. The ribs are then sawn off and the sternal plate or anterior chest wall is cut away, to expose the organs underneath. The most common way to remove the organs is known as the Rokitansky method. Organs are removed by cutting off their connections to the body and are usually removed as one.

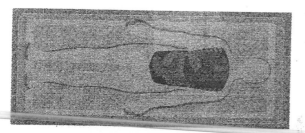

4. The brain is removed using a transverse incision (in a crosswise direction) through the brainstem, cutting the connection from the base of the brain to the spinal cord. The brain is then either cut fresh or is placed in a 20% solution of formalin to fix it for future analysis.

Fixing the brain

In cases like homicide or where there is a complex pathology of the brain, a detailed study of the brain may be necessary. In its fresh state the brain is very difficult to cut, so in order to make it easier for the neuropathologist to examine, the brain will be fixed in a solution of formalin for up to two weeks. Although two weeks is the optimal time to fix the brain, it can be sufficiently fixed in a shorter period in order to facilitate the return of the brain to the body prior to burial in selected cases.

Should the pathologist need to retain the whole brain it would typically be discussed with the relatives of the deceased first, prior to the release of the body for the funeral.

Once the study of the brain has been completed the brain would either be returned to the body, or in the case where the funeral has already taken place the pathologist will consult with the family to determine the most appropriate manner of disposing of the brain.

5. All removed organs are weighed and studied individually. Most organs are cut up in sections by a scalpel.

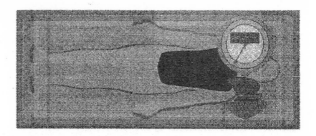

6. Intestines are drained in a sink to remove undigested food and faeces that remains.

7. The stomach is cut open on its greater curvature and the contents are examined.

8. Microscopic samples of most organs are taken for further analysis.

9. Finally, all major blood vessels are cut open and examined lengthwise.

10. The organs are placed back in the body, and the body will sometimes be filled with a filler material. The head and body are then sewn up. The brain is returned to the body, except in the cases where the brain has been retained for further tests.

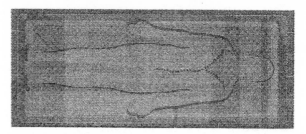

11. Once the Y incision is sewn up, the autopsy (without brain and tissue analysis) is complete.

Since there are three different levels of autopsy, under which circumstances do they apply? I have found that many families finds out after the autopsy that everything was said to have been destroyed. The brain, heart, and other body parts and fluids that are removed are classified as medical waste which generally means they are incinerated. I strongly feel the destruction of all internal organs which could determine the actual cause of death is a violation of family's rights. I guarantee if families are aware that everything would be destroyed during an autopsy they would not approve of this. How can a second opinion successfully be made if everything is destroyed during the initial autopsy? Do you think I would have paid $975 for a re-autopsy knowing there was nothing there to re-examine? So families, exercise your rights to be informed.

When I learned there were no marks on James neck followed by all of his organs and tissues, blood and brain being missing, I knew this was a cover up attempt. The only evidence we have left is the external evidence. Therefore James casket was placed in a volt to try to preserve the external evidence in the event that his body is exhumed. I tried to contact Mr. Michael Baden from HBO autopsy who specializes in examining dead bodies. Unfortunately since this was not a high profile case and no one legally felt we had sufficient evidence of a wrong doing, Mr. Baden was unable to assist in re-examining James body. So medically and officially, the 2 inch abrasion noted and documented on the right upper lateral part of James chin confirms that he died from a self inflicted partial suspension hanging from a bed sheet.

When the coroner listed everything that he was sending to me, it was all there except the "formal forensic photography taken prior to autopsy." I did not receive the photographs I had requested of James' neck. I did not tell the coroner that we had photographed the neck immediately after James was pronounced dead because I wanted him to show me the cards he held in his hands first. I wanted to compare notes. That is why I kept questioning everybody initially involved with James' body about what marks they saw on his neck. Since the coroner was summoned to the Sarah Bush Lincoln Health Center to tend to James' death, he should have at least looked at him and had to perform some kind of external examination.

OFFICE OF THE CORONER
COLES COUNTY

MICHAEL C. NICHOLS
County Coroner
e-mail: Coroner IL@AOL.COM

1 Western Ave Hgts.
Mattoon IL. 61938
Phone: (217) 234-2222
Or (217) 234-8013
Fax: (217) 258-6059

5th Vice-President: I. C. & M. E.

Date: January 21, 2001

To; The Dawson Family

Re: James Dawson,   Case # 2000-374
As per your request, I am enclosing a COPY FOR YOUR PERSONAL USE ONLY for examining the records in this case. Included in this transmittal is my Preliminary Report. This is where I was summoned to come to the Sarah Bush Lincoln Health Center Emergency Room regarding a death that had just been transported in by Toledo Ambulance. Next are copies of the Emergency Room Record depicting history of the case as examined by Dr Thomas Czelatdko, D.O. upon arrival to the Emergency Room. The next item is a copy of the Forensic Autopsy Report and performed by Dr. Travis Hindman at the Springfield Medical Center. This gives a detailed description of the procedure and examination, including Toxicology and the formal Forensic Photography take n prior to time of Autopsy. The next and last item in this packet is a PERSONAL COPY of the Transcript from the proceedings of the hearing that took place on December 20, 2000 at Mattoon City Hall Council Chambers.

One item to be addressed regarding the disposition of organs after Autopsy, and that it is standard practice to cremate the removed body parts after an Autopsy. To the best of my knowledge, this is standard practice for the disposal of all organs and tissue that were removed during time of Autopsy. At my hospital (Sarah Bush Lincoln Health Center) this has been the norm ever since I have been in this office. Should you inquire at other locations, I am sure you will find this to be in most all cases the Standard Operating Procedure.

Michael C. Nichols, CORONER
Coles County Illinois

The coroner stated there was one item to be addressed regarding the disposition of organs after autopsy, and that to the best of his knowledge, it was standard practice to cremate the removed body parts after autopsy.

*** Come on now. To the best of his knowledge? Is he serious? Getting rid of all internal evidence as to the actual cause of death should have been a known fact, not "to the best of his knowledge." ***

He stated that at his hospital (the Sarah Bush Lincoln Health Center) such had been the norm ever since he had been there.

*** Hold up, wait a minute. I thought the autopsy had been performed at the Memorial Medical Center in Springfield. Why was the coroner talking about normal procedures during autopsy at Sarah Bush Lincoln Health Center? James' body was supposed to have been transported to Springfield, per the coroner's request. So you mean to tell me they cremated all James' organs and tissues, including his brain, without notification and without authorization from the family, and it's legal? This is the law? What kind of laws are we governed by here? What happened to the autopsy procedure in which the brain and organs are put back in the body and small tissue samples are selected for microscopic examinations? Procedure states that if a pathologist needs to retain the whole brain, it is typically discussed with the family first. Since the coroner is so certain about the normal operating procedures at Sarah Bush Lincoln Health Center, I contacted them, and here is what they had to say:

Sarah Bush Lincoln Health Systems

Peggy Clark, R.N.
Patient Representative
1000 Health Center Drive
Mattoon, IL 61938
217-258/348-2491

Dear Ms. Dawson:

Many of the questions you have posed to me are beyond my scope of knowledge. I would suggest that questions pertaining to autopsy and cremation of organs be referred to a pathologist.

I understand from your first correspondence that you have copies of all of James' records. The information there should answer any other questions you have. Again, I extend my deepest sympathy to you and your family.

Sincerely,

Peggy Clark, RN

Peggy Clark, R.N.
Patient Representative

The way this letter sounds, you would think there was no pathologist at Sarah Bush Lincoln Health Center. So I contacted the Office of the Coroner once again, and here is what he had say:

February 25, 2001

Margaret A Dawson

Dear Margaret

I will try to answer your questions to your satisfaction and hope this will resolve any further inquiries from my office.

As far as the death summary, and noting all of the notifications of call order, yes the ROBI (Regional Organ Bank of Illinois) was notified. This is according to law that they be notified on any and all deaths that fall within the confines of the hospital. As far has James being a suitable donor, there was that possibility, but due to the nature of the death, that was not possible. There was an ongoing investigation into his death and if it had been allowed, this would have prevented a thorough investigation by autopsy as to the cause of death. First of all, had there been natural circumstances regarding James's death, there would have to be family consent given for him to be a donor. Margaret, this is just the law that ROBI be notified regarding his death.

As far as donating organs after autopsy, that is totally out of the question because the organs were dissected so they can be microscopically examined. There was a Forensic Autopsy performed at Memorial Medical Center in Springfield and not at Sarah Bush Lincoln Health Center. As far as the organs being cremated/incinerated; this has been the common practice of this facility for the past 50 years.

There is notation of the mark beneath the chin in the **summary page** of the **autopsy report**, but no exact measurements were given on this report other than noted of marks made by a bed sheet under the chin.

The cause of death, listed asphyxia secondary to hanging is when oxygen and blood flow is restricted in the neck, and in this case by a bed sheet.

I hope this has answered your questions regarding your tragic loss.

Respectfully yours

Michael C. Nichols
Coroner, Coles County Illinois

The coroner appears a little frustrated with my many questions, but that's okay because my family needed answers and, more importantly, some closure.

The coroner stated, "As far as the death summary, yes, the Regional Organ Bank of Illinois was notified; this is the law. They must be notified on all deaths that fall within the confines of the hospital. As far as James being a suitable donor, there was that possibility."

***Okay, I have no problems with the Regional Organ Bank of Illinois being contacted. My problem is that nobody told the family, who were right there on the premises, they was being contacted. Nobody asked the family about James' information, and I know more than his name needed to be reported to the Regional Organ Bank of Illinois. James was brought into the hospital wearing only his underwear and socks, so he did not have any of his information on him. His information had to come from the jail. James did not have his driver's license on him, but he had his state I.D., and on his state I.D., he is listed as an organ donor. ***

The coroner stated that, due to the nature of James' death, it was not possible for him to be an organ donor.

*** Who says it was not possible? All organs, all tissues, and all blood were taken. Are we supposed to believe everything was cremated just because the coroner said so? I don't think so. With the high demand for black market organs, who's to say the organs weren't stolen, sold, and transplanted? For whom was James suitable? The coroner and the pathologist left the door wide open to such possibilities when they decided to take everything from James' cavity. ***

The coroner stated that donating organs after autopsy was out of the question because the organs were dissected so they could be microscopically examined.

*** I know organs cannot be donated after they are dissected. So you mean to tell me all organs were dissected and microscipally examined then cremated?***

The coroner stated that had there been natural circumstances resulting in James' death, there would have had to be a family's consent for him to be a donor.

***Okay, then why isn't a family's consent needed to take and cremate all organs? ***

The coroner stated that the forensic autopsy was performed at the Memorial Medical Center in Springfield, not at Sarah Bush Lincoln Health Center.

Hey, he was the one who started talking about the standard operating procedure during autopsy at Sarah Bush Lincoln Health Center, not me.

The coroner stated that as far as organs being cremated/ incinerated, it had been the common practice of this facility for the past fifty years.

***Therefore, every autopsy performed at the Memorial Medical Center in Springfield and the Sarah Bush Lincoln Health Center in Mattoon for the past fifty years consisted of cremating everything from the internal cavity, including the brain, without notification and authorization from the families? Does the record show that? ***

The coroner stated that there was a notation of the mark made beneath the chin in the summary of the autopsy report. I asked the coroner what marks he personally witnessed on James' neck, and he told me what the autopsy documents, an autopsy his counterpart pathologist in Springfield performed. Here is a little history on the Memorial Medical Center in Springfield:

Location: *Springfield Illinois* | Category: *Hospitals and Medical Centers*

 Memorial Medical Center

The department of laboratory and Pathology at the Memorial Medical Center is a full service laboratory offering a broad range of routine and specialty services both inpatient and outpatient medical care. The laboratory is active in providing educational opportunities for both medical students and resident physicians at the SIU School of Medicine and Clinical Laboratory Science Education for medical technologists in affiliation with University of Illinois in Springfield. Over 160 medical technologists and laboratory support personnel staff the Central Illinois, Ltd/Clinical Pathologists of Central Illinois, Ltd. Thirteen pathologists provide a broad range of expertise in both clinical and anatomic pathology. Each department of laboratory is directed by a pathologist and registered medical technologist. The laboratory is accredited by the College of American Pathologist. (CAP) The American Association of Blood Banks (AABB) and holds a CLIA (Clinical Laboratory Improvement Act) certified from Health Care Finance Administration. The laboratory offers a broad range of routine and specialty services in each of the following department:

.Blood Bank	.Immunology
.Chemistry/Urinalysis	.Immino-transplant (histocompatibility)
.Coagulation	laboratory
.Cytology	.Microbiology
	.Surgical and Anatomic Pathology

I sent a letter twice to the Regional Organ Bank of Illinois, questioning them about the suitable donor decision documented in James' medical records. Unfortunately, they decided not to respond. Here is the copy of proof of delivery, followed by the letter:

received February 20, 2002

SENDER: COMPLETE THIS SECTION	COMPLETE THIS SECTION ON DELIVERY
■ Complete items 1, 2, and 3. Also complete item 4 if Restricted Delivery is desired. ■ Print your name and address on the reverse so that we can return the card to you. ■ Attach this card to the back of the mailpiece, or on the front if space permits.	A. Signature X _Roy McGlul_ ☐ Agent ☐ Addressee B. Received by (Printed Name) C. Date of Delivery 2-20-02
1. Article Addressed to: Regional Organ Bank of Illinois 1 West Old State Capital Plaza Suite 711 Springfield Ill 62701	D. Is delivery address different from item 1? ☐ Yes If YES, enter delivery address below: ☐ No
	3. Service Type ☐ Certified Mail ☐ Express Mail ☐ Registered ☐ Return Receipt for Merchandise ☐ Insured Mail ☐ C.O.D. 4. Restricted Delivery? (Extra Fee) ☐ Yes
2. Article Number (Transfer from service label) 7001-1940-8974-0037	

PS Form 3811, August 2001   Domestic Return Receipt

received March 11, 2002

SENDER: COMPLETE THIS SECTION	COMPLETE THIS SECTION ON DELIVERY
■ Complete items 1, 2, and 3. Also complete item 4 if Restricted Delivery is desired. ■ Print your name and address on the reverse so that we can return the card to you. ■ Attach this card to the back of the mailpiece, or on the front if space permits.	A. Signature X _Roy McGlul_ ☐ Agent ☐ Addressee B. Received by (Printed Name) C. Date of Delivery 3-11-02
1. Article Addressed to: Regional Organ Bank of Illinois Suite 711 1 West Old State Capital Plaza Springfield Ill 62701	D. Is delivery address different from item 1? ☐ Yes If YES, enter delivery address below: ☐ No
	3. Service Type ☐ Certified Mail ☐ Express Mail ☐ Registered ☐ Return Receipt for Merchandise ☐ Insured Mail ☐ C.O.D. 4. Restricted Delivery? (Extra Fee) ☐ Yes
2. Article Number (Transfer from service label) 7001 1940 0005 8974 8359	

Regional Organ Bank of Illinois
1 West Old State Capital Plaza
Suite 711
Springfield, Ill. 62701

RE: Suitable donor decision made by your establishment.
Transplant Coordinator Brendan Glynn #0040373

To any supervisor or whomever it may concern:

I, Margaret (Dawson) Brown, am writing in regards to the Death Summary document located in the medical records of James Dawson. I have enclosed a copy of this document for you to review. On November 6, 2000, at 13:45 (1:45 p.m.) a call was made to your establishment reporting the death of James Dawson from the Sarah Bush Lincoln Health Center, located in Mattoon, Illinois. My question is who reported James Dawson's death to your establishment?

Unfortunately, James did not have any of his personal identification on him in order for his information to have been passed on to your establishment, and I am quite sure more than his name needed to be reported. Although the Death Summary document is incomplete, because a suitable donor decision has been checked off then the body of James Dawson arrived back to his family a completely empty cavity, something is definitely wrong here.

I realize your establishment has absolutely nothing to do with the missing organs or any of the bizarre circumstances surrounding James' death; however, we would like to know who gave transplant coordinator Brendan Glynn #0040373, James Dawson's information. Any information your establishment is able to provide at this time would be greatly appreciated.

In Springfield, organs, tissues, and blood donors are the focus of the Office of the Secretary of State. Right next door, their neighbors are cremating organs. It states, "Currently thousands of people in Illinois and around the world are in need of an organ and tissue transplant. Without it, many will die, but you can help. You can become an organ donor and give someone a second chance at life. The most important thing to remember is to tell your family about your wishes because hospitals always require the next of kin's consent before donations can occur. Tell your families because hospitals will not be able to remove any organs or tissues without permission from the donor's family. The donor registry is a computerized database that documents your loved one's wishes regarding donation. This registry provides valuable information to families who are asked at the hospital for consent to donate. Does the registry replace the donor card on the back of your driver's license or state I.D? No! This registry is meant as a supplement, not a replacement to the uniform organ donor card. But either action still depends on the consent of the next of kin before any organs can be removed. "Let's go to why James' license was suspended. I contacted the Office of the Secretary of State to inquire on the status of James' driver's license and to request a copy of it. Here is what I found:

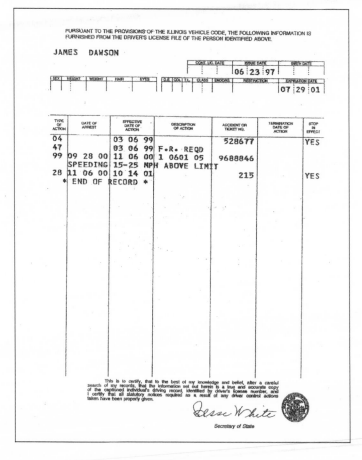

Accident or Ticket Number 528677 Stop in Effect Yes

Description of Action F.R. REQD.

I was informed by a representative from the Office of the Secretary of State that the above two transactions says that James was involved in a fender bender and had provided no proof of insurance on the vehicle he was operating. He was given a date to appear in court, which is the Date of Action 03-06-99. He appeared in court and provided proof of insurance, but the proof of insurance was for after the incident. Therefore, he was given a fine, which he paid, and he was placed under supervision. *Description of Action F.R. REQD* means, "Future insurance required." Although James did provide proof of insurance, he needed to have repurchased the SR-22 insurance because he was under supervision. This policy reports financial responsibility for insurance to the Office of the Secretary of State. James was unaware of the stipulation surrounding the SR-22 because he still had the same insurance policy he had purchased since his court date on 03-06-99. Unfortunately, this policy does not report your financial responsibility to the Office of the Secretary of State. Due to the wrong insurance coverage while under supervision, James' license continued to be suspended.

"Type of Action 99, Date of Arrest 09-28-00." *Date of Arrest* also refers to the date the citation was issued. This is the day James' friend talked about in his letter when James was stopped for speeding. The officer told James his license was suspended for lack of SR-22 insurance, so even though he provided proof of insurance, the officer still had to cite him. The officer took his license, gave him a ticket, and told him that he could drive on the ticket; however, he had to report to court on 11-6-00 to straighten out his suspension. *(1 0601)* means, "Conviction for speeding" and *(05)* means, "Financial responsibility suspension." "Accident or Ticket number 9688846, Speeding 15-25 miles above the limit."

James was stopped for the same thing on 11-05-00, only this time, he was arrested and taken to the Cumberland County jail. He was driving on a ticket, so the officer who stopped him should have been aware of the court date he had the following day. I imagine this was just one stop too many. *Type of Action 28* means, "Reported deceased." When I read the date of arrest was 11-06-00, I assumed it was for the citation issued to James on the night of 11-05-00. I was told this transaction was documented because James did not report to court on his scheduled court date, which ironically, is the same day he died. "Effective Date of Action 10-14-01" is the day I reported James' death to the Office of the Secretary of State and requested a copy of his driver's record. Ticket No. 215 and Stop in Effect means since James did not report to court on November 6, a warrant was being placed on him. You will clearly observe from James' driver's record that when he was stopped on September 28, there was no Stop in Effect, there was no warrant. This ends the transactions made on James' driver's record. I explained to the representative from the Office of the Secretary of State that James had been taken to jail on the night of 11-05-00 and had died the next day. I asked if his death meant the citation issued to him that night would not be documented on his driver's record. I was told that James' death had nothing to do with the citation issued to him the day before. Once an officer stops a person and cites him or her, it had to be logged by that officer. So according to the Office of the Secretary of State and James' driver's record, no citation was issued to him on the night of November 5, 2000. This is why in my letter to Ms. Maryland Huckaby, I requested the name of the arresting officer. I wanted to know what happened to the citation he supposedly issued.

Notifications of suspensions are not sent by certified letters and do not require proof of delivery. If the stipulations and the ramifications behind the offense cited are not clearly understood while one is in that courtroom, one may not be aware of these stipulations, especially if one has insurance on one's vehicle and the record shows otherwise.

After my brother's death, I decided to keep his vehicle since it was the last place he was alive. Sentimental reasons alone led me to arrange with the financing company to pay the vehicle off and have the title and registration changed to my name. As I waited on the transaction to be finalized, I kept my brother's vehicle in my garage because I have my own vehicle as well. About two months after my brother's death I decided to drive his car to go get something to eat. Sure enough, I'm driving in that Grand Am, listening to music, and my mind was nowhere on the speed limit. I was driving through my neighborhood, a route I take daily, and I was stopped for speeding. I was doing 47 in a 35-mph zone. The officer checked my license and told me to slow down. However, in most suburban areas, when an officer stops you, another usually comes right along. When the other officer arrived, I was asked for proof of insurance and the vehicle registration. I went to the glove compartment, pulled the information out, and gave it to the officer. Even after showing James' insurance information, they checked the car's plates and they came up suspended, and James' SR-22 suspension popped up. They actually took the license plates off the vehicle. I explained about my brother's death and the transaction being made on the vehicle. Although it was an interesting conversation, the officer still had to cite me. The next day, I added my brother's vehicle to my insurance policy. I went to court and provided proof of insurance, but the proof of insurance was after the incident. I had to pay a fine, and I was placed under supervision. When I left the courtroom, I thought that was the end of it. However, three months later, I received a letter from the Office of the Secretary of State for notice of suspension. I immediately called their office because I just knew they had made a huge mistake. I was told that since I was under supervision, I needed to purchase an SR-22 insurance policy. This was the first I'd ever heard about an SR-22. It should have been brought to my attention when I was in that courtroom. What if I hadn't received the letter or read it? I would have been driving around, unaware my license had been suspended. So please be aware of the status of your driver's license after any citation, and please be aware of the status of the vehicle you are operating. Although our intentions are to just get in a vehicle and go from one place to another, anything can happen in between, and nobody needs to be hauled off to jail for a traffic violation. In 1999, the mandatory insurance law was strictly enforced, and I'm quite sure the stipulation surrounding the SR-22 got many people in trouble with the law. Now everybody knows about it. It was ironic that I personally experienced why my brother's license continued to be suspended while I was compiling this documentary about his death. That is what I call some kind of coincidence.

Incidentally, going through the glove compartment of my brother's vehicle, I found several documents that do not appear to be the actions of someone contemplating suicide. I found a cleaner's ticket. He had prepaid for his clothes to be cleaned, which I picked up. I found $14 worth of lottery tickets he purchased for 11-5-00, the same night he was taken to jail. I found Yale insurance receipts for his car insurance payments, the last one being for 10-17-00. I found a Midas receipt for brake repairs he paid cash for on 11-3-00. A pair of timberland boots he had ordered arrived on the day of his funeral. In addition, he paid for a trip to Las Vegas for New Years. You may now review some of those documents:

```
     PICK  4                    PICK  4

     EVENING                    EVENING

7834  STR      .50         7834  BOX      .50

  SUN NOV05 00   $   0.50     SUN NOV05 00   $   0.50
    134213      08126           134213      08126
  LOTTO  11/08/00  $2 MILL    LOTTO  11/08/00  $2 MILL
  BIG GM 11/07/00  $18 MILL   BIG GM 11/07/00  $18 MILL

   034561 310-09987001-146      033653 310-16016277-206
```


```
     PICK  4                    PICK  4

     EVENING                    EVENING

7834  STR     1.00         5237  STR     1.00

  SUN NOV05 00   $   1.00     SUN NOV05 00   $   1.00
    134213      08126           134213      08126
  LOTTO  11/08/00  $2 MILL    LOTTO  11/08/00  $2 MILL
  BIG GM 11/07/00  $18 MILL   BIG GM 11/07/00  $18 MILL

   034397 310-13002311-031      035076 310-16410171-083
```

```
         PICK  4                    PICK  4

       EVENING                    EVENING

    3983  BOX   .50           3983  STR   .50

     SUN NOV05 00   $  0.50      SUN NOV05 00   $  0.50
       134213     08126           134213     08126
     LOTTO 11/08/00  $2 MILL     LOTTO 11/08/00  $2 MILL
     BIG GM 11/07/00 $18 MILL    BIG GM 11/07/00 $18 MILL

      038901 310-14444349-175     038858 310-10643427-008
```

```
         PICK  4                    PICK  4

       EVENING                    EVENING

    5926  BOX   .50           5926  STR   .50

     SUN NOV05 00   $  0.50      SUN NOV05 00   $  0.50
       134213     08126           134213     08126
     LOTTO 11/08/00  $2 MILL     LOTTO 11/08/00  $2 MILL
     BIG GM 11/07/00 $18 MILL    BIG GM 11/07/00 $18 MILL

      032691 310-09528640-162     032807 310-09265820-193
```

PICK 4

EVENING

8716 BOX .50

SUN NOV05 00 $ 0.50

134213 08126

LOTTO 11/08/00 $2 MILL
BIG GM 11/07/00 $18 MILL

036428 310-14967941-048

PICK 4

EVENING

8716 STR .50

SUN NOV05 00 $ 0.50

134213 08126

LOTTO 11/08/00 $2 MILL
BIG GM 11/07/00 $18 MILL

035689 310-15557884-205

PICK 3

EVENING

769 STRBX 1.00

SUN NOV05 00 $ 1.00

134213 08126

LOTTO 11/08/00 $2 MILL
BIG GM 11/07/00 $18 MILL

039485 310-10190378-182

PICK 3

EVENING

818 STRBX 1.00

SUN NOV05 00 $ 1.00

134213 08126

LOTTO 11/08/00 $2 MILL
BIG GM 11/07/00 $18 MILL

035918 310-16146551-003

PICK 4

EVENING

5237   STR   .50

SUN NOV05 00 $ 0.50
   134213   08126
LOTTO 11/08/00 $2 MILL
BIG GM 11/07/00 $18 MILL

035237 310-11297485-180

PICK 4

EVENING

5237   BOX   .50

SUN NOV05 00 $ 0.50
   134213   08126
LOTTO 11/08/00 $2 MILL
BIG GM 11/07/00 $18 MILL

035215 310-10642147-130

PICK 4

EVENING

4128   BOX   .50

SUN NOV05 00 $ 0.50
   134213   08126
LOTTO 11/08/00 $2 MILL
BIG GM 11/07/00 $18 MILL

038952 310-10576752-190

PICK 4

EVENING

4128   STR   .50

SUN NOV05 00 $ 0.50
   134213   08126
LOTTO 11/08/00 $2 MILL
BIG GM 11/07/00 $18 MILL

038905 310-12346205-135

```
       PICK  4                    PICK  4

      EVENING                    EVENING

   0326  BOX   .50            0326  STR   .50

   SUN NOV05 00    $  0.50      SUN NOV05 00    $  0.50
      134213      08126           134213      08126
   LOTTO  11/08/00   $2 MILL    LOTTO  11/08/00   $2 MILL
   BIG GM 11/07/00  $18 MILL    BIG GM 11/07/00  $18 MILL

   030049 310-16344488-075     030010 310-13657201-117
```

```
       PICK  4                    PICK  4

      EVENING                    EVENING

   1030  BOX   .50            1030  STR   .50

   SUN NOV05 00    $  0.50      SUN NOV05 00    $  0.50
      134213      08126           134213      08126
   LOTTO  11/08/00   $2 MILL    LOTTO  11/08/00   $2 MILL
   BIG GM 11/07/00  $18 MILL    BIG GM 11/07/00  $18 MILL

   034558 310-10903719-050     034743 310-12804338-147
```

151

PICK 3   PICK 3

EVENING   EVENING

609 STRBX 1.00   481 STRBX 1.00

SUN NOV05 00 $ 1.00   SUN NOV05 00 $ 1.00
134213   08126   134213   08126
LOTTO 11/08/00 $2 MILL   LOTTO 11/08/00 $2 MILL
BIG GM 11/07/00 $18 MILL   BIG GM 11/07/00 $18 MILL

031206 310-15695518-179   035082 310-12812018-175

YOUR CURRENCY EXCHANGE

CHECKS CASHED
GAS, LABEL, PHONE & TAXES
BILLS ACCEPTED FOR PAYMENT
NOTARY PUBLIC
AUTO & DRIVER LICENSE SERVICE
INCOME TAX SERVICE

COMMUNITY SERVICE CENTER   2-250 / 710   0

9250 SO. COTTAGE GROVE - CHICAGO, ILLINOIS 60619

PHONE 773-487-0040

CORUS BANK
CHICAGO, ILLINOIS

No. P 839886

10/17/00

REMITTER *James Dawson*

PAY TO THE ORDER OF *Yale Insurance*

$$206.00

COTTAGE - 83RD CURRENCY EXCHANGE INC.

STATE REGULATED

Two Hundred Six & 00/100 U.S. Dollars

not Valid Over $$ 300.00 NO REFUND IF LOST IN BLANK 0.05 MHF *839886*

NOT VALID OVER $ 1000.00
REPLACEMENT OF THIS INSTRUMENT, IF NECESSARY, WILL BEGIN 30 DAYS AFTER THE PURCHASE DATE. THERE WILL BE A FEE CHARGED FOR THIS SERVICE.
THE PURCHASER OF THIS INSTRUMENT AGREES TO INSERT THE NAME OF THE PAYEE AND ASSUMES TOTAL RESPONSIBILITY FOR ANY EVENTS MADE POSSIBLE BY FAILURE TO DO SO.

As I Travel Through the Valley of Death

```
                    Midas Auto Systems Experts
              1717-23 N. Clybourn - Chicago, IL 60614
                         312/642/0455

MIDAS

                      * * I N V O I C E * *

Date: 11-03-00  Time: 16:32:45   Invoice #: 542158   Estimate #: 1014000

   Name: JAMES DAWSON                              Cash:     143.21
Address:                                           Check:      0.00
     : CHICAGO              IL                      Charge:     0.0?
  Phone:                                            Acct:
                                                   PO #:
Vehicle: PONTIAC GRAND AM 1999                        :       0.00
   VIN:                                                :       0.00
  Plate: J546058   Mileage In: 39464   Out: 39464

Facility #: 100440        Salesperson:  1/  0
Installers: B:4:BARRETO, R

  Qty  Part Number   Description              Cd Pr.Each   Labor  Ext.Amt
--BRAKES:
    1  BP1738        PRO SERIES PADS           R   50.99   72.32  123.31

    2  BR001         RECONDITION ROTOR - OFF CA LR  18.00  18.00   36.00
  Tax    3.90      0.00       0.00              Total BRAKES   159.31

                                               Total Parts     50.99
  Tax  STATE                                   Total Labor    108.32
       3.90      0.00       0.00                Total Tax       3.90
                                        Less SALE Discount     20.00
                                              Grand Total     143.21
```

We at Midas want to be your Auto Systems Experts. We trust you are satisfied with the quality of our products, service, and workmanship. If, for some reason, you are not satisfied, please call:

TIM FLOSS (630) 627-7906

All parts used in repairing your car are new unless otherwise specified.

SERVICE MANAGER:

11-03-2000

PLEASE READ REVERSE SIDE FOR WARRANTY INFORMATION
THIS INVOICE DOES NOT REPLACE YOUR GUARANTEE.   542158

153

Searching for Justice

After meeting with Attorney Hopson on November 17, 2000, I thought it was a perfect opportunity for me to put my secretarial skills and my want-to-be lawyer skills to use. I started compiling as much incriminating evidence as I could. I compiled all of my information in this documentary, which I call my case file. The case never even got lukewarm; it stayed as cold as James' hand was when Mom touched him.

I appeared on the talk radio station WVON (1450 AM) with Monique Smith four times discussing the unusual circumstances surrounding my brother's death. It was a beautiful experience. I shared my story, but I ended up receiving much more than I could have ever given. Monique's audience brought me more strength than I knew I had. Listening to the many people who had lost loved ones in jail the same way as James was overwhelming. I was completely unaware an epidemic of this nature even existed. Several people called in whose loved ones were taken to jail for a suspended license then later found hanging. I could not believe it. How can someone go from driving on a suspended license to hanging? With all of this hanging going on, a suspended license seems dead serious. I thought lynchings and hangings only existed in the past, but they are just as alive today.

Sharing my story on the air brought a little attention from the media, which I appreciated. We listen to the media. I received a phone call from Ms. Memorie Knox of *Final Call,* which led to two stories being printed in their publications. Ms. Knox and the entire *Final Call* organization were wonderful and very supportive. I thank Ms. Monique Smith of WVON and Ms. Memorie Knox of *Final Call* for their dedication and help in bringing forth justice in our wrongful death claim. Here are the two articles printed in *Final Call*:

The Final Call

DECEMBER 5, 2000

THE FINAL CALL

Family suspects foul play by rural cops
Man's body returned to family without blood, body parts

by Memorie Knox

CHICAGO—A full investigation is underway surrounding the mysterious death of a Black man who was arrested for driving with a suspended license and allegedly hung himself in a rural jail while waiting for his family to post bail.

The family of James Dawson, a 37-year-old parking attendant, have reason to suspect a cover-up and are questioning where and why all of the blood and organs were removed from the body without their permission.

Margo Brown said her brother was last seen Nov. 5 leaving his parents' home on the city's south side in his 1999 gray Pontiac Grand Am car at approximately 6 p.m. Mr. Dawson's planned destination is uncertain.

Ms. Brown said her mother, Lillie Dawson, received a call from her son around 2:17 a.m. on Nov. 6 saying he was being detained at the Cumberland County Correctional Facility (225 miles south of Chicago) after being pulled over by police for speeding. Mr. Dawson informed his mother that police ran a check on his license and he was told it was suspended. He was arrested, taken to jail and bail was set at $150.

Mrs. Dawson, her son and grandson arrived at the facility around noon. After posting bail, Ms. Brown said the clerk told the family to wait outside in the car and that Mr. Dawson

James Dawson—suicide or murder

would exit through a door close to the parking lot.

Soon, Ms. Brown said, an ambulance pulled up and the clerk came out of the building and informed the family that the apparent medical emergency would delay Mr. Dawson's release for at least another 15 minutes. However, family members contend they were not told that the medical emergency was Mr. Dawson.

"I'm sure the clerk knew the ambulance was there for my brother because he was the only Black inmate, out of eight total, in the jail," Ms. Brown said.

When emergency medical technicians (EMT) came out of the facility, the family noticed that Mr. Dawson was lying on the gurney. Mrs. Dawson immediately jumped out of the car, rushed to her son's side and held his hand, which she describes as "cold as ice." Mrs. Dawson questioned his condition

and an EMT suggested that she trail them to a local hospital. For the next 20 minutes the family followed the ambulance, which traveled the speed limit and without sirens—only flashing lights.

Mr. Dawson was pronounced dead upon arrival.

After viewing the remains, the grandson asked the nurse about the abrasion on Mr. Dawson's chin and questioned the cause of death. The grandson was told that Mr. Dawson hung himself with a belt. When he informed the nurse that his uncle was last seen wearing a black jogging suit, she said paperwork revealed that Mr. Dawson used a shower curtain. The nurse also confirmed that there were no marks on the victim's neck, according to the family.

The Dawsons traveled back to jail and received the bail money and a bag with Mr. Dawson's belongings, which included his clothes. The grandson asked the clerk why Mr. Dawson was taken away in the ambulance wearing only his underwear and the clerk said he was taking a shower. He also questioned where in the shower was his uncle found. The clerk said he was found hanging in his cell with sheets, according to the family.

"There were so many conflicting stories that it sounded suspi-

Continued on page 10

Hanging

Continued from page 5

sious. If someone is found hanging in your jail, you should know exactly what object was found around their neck. We should not have been told two and three different objects. "Ms Brown" said.

The family was told that an autopsy had to be done at a nearby hospital before the body could be transported to Chicago. Ms. Brown said. After the autopsy was completed, A.R. Leak's and Sons Funeral directors called the Dawson's home to question whether Mr. Dawson's body was where it was suppose to be because they had been given the run-around. The funeral home did not receive the body until the following day.

Special agent Kelly Hodge of the Illinois State Police told the Final Call that a coroner's inquest and jury will determine whether the case is a homicide or suicide.

An independent autopsy ordered by the family revealed no signs of a struggle. The pathologist told the family that the cause of death was strangulation and that the body was healthy, but contained no blood or organs.

The Dawson has immediately retained a lawyer with the firm of renowned Black attorney Johnnie Cochran to begin an investigation. Ms. Brown said Toledo Ill, investigators told the family they saw no signs of foul play and observed the jail's surveillance on the day in question. Investigators said no one entered Mr. Dawson's cell while incarcerated. At 11:05 a.m., they said another inmate saw Mr. Dawson laying down and at 11:20 a.m. a Correctional Officer saw him laying down. The family asked when did Mr. Dawson allegedly remove his clothes and hang himself, but they got no clear answer.

Ms. Brown said the last call her brother made on his cell phone was to a friend at 11:00. The call was before he was stopped by the police.

Our family is strong and we believe that eventually some information will be given to find out exactly what happened. There is no way he would hang himself and he was only in jail for a traffic violation. It's not like he was about to be sentenced or anything. It was just for a traffic violation. Ms. Brown said.

The family said the independent pathologist is conducting more tests and the results are scheduled to be revealed in December. The official police report and death certificate have not been released, the family said.

Missing organs, conflicting stories?

Victim's family has new questions about Illinois jail house 'suicide' report

by Memorie Knox

CHICAGO—The family of a Black man whose death was deemed suicide by 12 white jurors and whose internal organs were cremated without the family's permission, believe their loved one's death was a cover-up, and are now calling on the FBI to conduct a full investigation.

According to Margaret Brown, her brother, James Dawson, a 37-year-old parking attendant, was pronounced dead on arrival on November 6, 2000 at the Sarah Bushlincoln Health Center in Springfield, Ill. Ms. Brown said the divorcee and father of one son was last seen on Nov. 5, 2000 leaving his parents' home in Chicago in his 1999 gray Pontiac Grand Am, heading for an unknown destination.

That night, Ms. Brown said, her mother, Lillie Dawson, received a call from her brother saying he had been pulled over by police near Toledo, for speeding, was informed that his license had been suspended, and was being detained at the Cumberland County Correctional Facility (225 miles south of Chicago). Bail was set at $150.

Ms. Brown said her mother, brother and grandson arrived at the facility around noon the next day and posted bail. While following the clerk's request for the family to wait outside in the parking lot, an ambulance pulled up outside of the building. The clerk came out to tell the family that the apparent medical emergency would detain Mr. Dawson's release for approximately

15 minutes, she said.

Family members contend they were not told that the medical emergency involved Mr. Dawson, who was the only Black out of eight inmates.

Ms. Brown said emergency medical technicians emerged from the facility carrying Mr. Dawson, who was wearing noting but his underwear. His mother rushed to his side, held his hand, which she described as "cold as ice," and was told to trail the ambulance when she asked questions about his condition. After 20 minutes of trailing the ambulance, which traveled the speed limit without sirens—only flashing lights—family members said they learned that Mr. Dawson was dead.

While the family made Mr. Dawson's funeral arrangements, they were questioned by the mortuary as to why all the internal organs had been extracted. Knowing that Mr. Dawson was not an organ donor, and that the coroner's report concluded that he hung himself, the family began to suspect foul play and immediately retained a lawyer.

Illinois state police began its investigation. Ms. Brown said, and on Dec. 20, 2000, an all white, 12-members jury, who heard the results of that investigation during a coroner's inquest, determined Mr. Dawson committed suicide.

During the inquest, Mr. Dawson's family members heard the testimony of the Springfield, Ill., pathologist, who said it was normal hospital procedure to cremate the organs after autopsy and that a small mark on Mr. Dawson's chin was evidence he hung himself.

Mr. Dawson's family said no marks were found on his neck.

Although the family attended the inquest, Ms. Brown said notification of the original hearing, set for early December, was sent to her parents' home with the wrong address.

Investigators were not expecting the family to attend, Ms. Brown said, and when they entered the courtroom, seven minutes after it began, a one-minute recess was called in the middle of testimony.

On March 7, the results of an investigation conducted by Black broadcast journalist and investigative reporter Renee Ferguson revealed jail officials told state police that he was found hanging from a shower pole with a sheet around his neck.

But Mr. Dawson was never issued a sheet and hung himself using a mattress pad, Ms. Ferguson's investigation revealed.

The results of Ms. Ferguson's investigation prompted the family to call the FBI.

"At first we thought it was an accident, but now it looks like murder, with accessory by the coroner. They cremated all of the evidence of a homicide. Without the organs, it is almost impossible to determine a cause of death. Now it's time for the FBI to get involved," Ms. Brown told *The Final Call.*

Ms. Brown said the family, which has filed a wrongful death lawsuit, will also seek new legal representation, saying their lawyer hasn't been involved enough in the case.

When I got up to fifty pages of incriminating evidence, I delivered copies of my findings to our attorney, the Rainbow Push Coalition, the Southside branch office of the NAACP, Judge Eugene Pincham, and other establishments, to no avail. Ms. Renee Ferguson, an investigative reporter from NBC Channel 5 News of Chicago, was one of the people I had contacted. Just like the others, she was reluctant to get involved with the case at first. She felt that perhaps, being the family, we just could not accept that maybe James did take his own life. It amazes me that when a jail staff presents a suicide, most people believe what they said happened. Again, their word is law, but when you know someone, I mean really know someone, no one can just tell you anything about them.

I stayed in contact with Ms. Ferguson, and talking to her was like being in a psychiatrist office. She was amazing. She gave me as much direction as she possibly could and she was always just a telephone call away. During the most crucial and difficult time, from November to March 2001, Ms. Ferguson went from an investigative reporter to my biggest supporter. She encouraged me to never give up in what I believed, no matter what it took. She taught me to dig deep and keep digging until there was no more dirt left. Ms. Ferguson was a guest speaker at Columbia College for the graduating class of 2001. She talked about my family's fight for justice in her speech, which brought great attention to our case. She helped paved the way and there was a little sunshine on a dark situation.

I thank Ms. Renee Ferguson with every breath I take because her input and professionalism was my greatest inspiration. Here is the news story held on March 7, 2001, on Channel 5, from Ms. Renee Ferguson:

NEARLY EVERY JOB ON THE WEB
careerbuilder SEARCH OVER 2,000,000 JOBS Unit

MSNBC Local
HOME LOCAL NEWS | LOCAL WEATHER | LOCAL SPORTS | MORE CITIES | WRITE US | NEXT STORY

News
Business
Sports
Local
Health
Technology
Living • Travel
TV News
Opinions
Weather
Shop@MSNBC
MSN.com

Chicago, IL **5**

Family questions suicide

by Renee Ferguson

CHICAGO, Mar 7. – A Chicago man is stopped for speeding, taken to jail and 12 hours later he is dead. Officials ruled the death a suicide, but James Dawson's family is asking for further investigation into the case.

Dawson's family say he was traveling to Tunica Mississippi to gamble when his plans hit a major roadblock in Downstate Illinois. Unit 5 investigated the death and discovered disturbing evidence which led to more questions. What *did* happen to James Dawson?

Records show that police stopped Dawson's car at 11:20 p.m. on November 5th as he drove south on I - 57. Three hours later, the Chicago resident called his mother, Lillie Dawson, from the Cumberland County jail in Toledo, Il. - 200 miles south of Chicago.

He said,"The police stopped me for speeding and they said my license was suspended," Mrs. Dawson recalls.

The following morning, Mrs. Dawson traveled to Toledo to bail out her son. When she arrived, she watched in disbelief as James was carried out of the jail on a stretcher. She touched her son's hand and "his hand was ice cold," she said. James was dead on arrival at the local emergency hospital.

According to official documents, jailers told State Police they found Dawson hanging from a shower pole with a bed sheet around his neck. But when Unit-5 discovered Dawson was never issued a sheet, official later said he hanged himself with a mattress pad.

Jeraldine Mosley-McCall works for Leak Funeral Home in Chicago, which handled Dawson's body. When she examined the remains she was shocked by what she saw. She said: "Everything from inside, it was an empty cavity...all of those organs were removed from that remains," Mosley-McCall said.

Unit 5 learned that all of James Dawson's internal organs were cremated after an autopsy by a Springfield pathologist. Unit 5 tried to contact the pathologist for more than a month, but he did not return our calls. The pathologist concluded that a mark on Dawson's chin was a ligature mark "evidence" he had hanged himself.

> Mosley-McCall questions that conclusion. "Generally if a person has caused their own death by hanging, there are bruises or contusions or something," she said.
>
> Investigative reporter Renee Ferguson show morgue photos of the body to an independent pathologist, Dr. James Bryant, who has performed more than 1,600 autopies during his 23 year career. Bryant did not conclude Dawson died by hanging.
>
> "You would see a kind of diffused bruising which you don't see here. All we have is a mark on the chin and that could be anything under the sun," Bryant said.
>
> "But because Dawson's organs were destroyed, Bryant added, it would be almost impossible for another pathologist to accurately examine the case. Without the organs, we are missing a few pieces" he said.
>
> The Dawson family is still looking for pieces of the puzzle to answer how James Dawson's life ended. They are considering exhuming the body and requesting a thorough investigation in this case.

About a week before Ms. Ferguson broke the story, our attorney informed us that he did not have enough evidence to start an investigation. I was in complete shock. I thought you had to investigate in order to get the evidence. We had wasted four months for absolutely nothing. I asked Attorney Hopson about the pictures we had given him. That wasn't enough? He told me the photographs were not admissible because there was no date on them. He told me I needed to try to obtain the official photographs from the coroner's office. I requested photographs of James' neck from the Springfield pathologist and the coroner. Of course, they did not send the photographs. Every question I threw at Attorney Hopson received a ridiculous answer. We were back at ground zero. Attorney Hopson was a young attorney, and he told us his instructions came straight from the head man, Mr. Montgomery. I understand that not every potential wrongful death claim that walks through the doors of our most powerful defense attorneys and civil rights organizations are going to leave with justice on their side. While we constantly hear about all the success in defending our rights for justice from the Cochran administration, the Rainbow Push Coalition, and the NAACP, what about the unsuccessful cases that are never talked about, never brought to the media's attention, and simply placed in their files of statistics?

When we are faced with unusual and suspicious circumstances surrounding the death of any human being, we look for justice. We look to the justice system to provide us with the rights we have fought so hard to receive. The right to challenge questionable circumstances in the death of a loved one is a human right. Our legal system is filled with individuals blessed to be prominent, successful attorneys. Civil rights organizations have carried us for decades on issues that have been successfully addressed. We have overcome so much in our struggle for justice, and I thank God for all who have contributed to that success. But for right now, it's not about what we overcame, it's about what we have yet to overcome that lies deep within my heart.

When justice falls above all that we know, what is there for us to do but seek legal assistance? However, when legal assistance fails and nobody wants to take their precious time to investigate the claim of a wrongful death, our journey can become a never-ending nightmare. It's different if somebody at least attempts to investigate a claim, but when a claim is completely ignored, how are we supposed to weigh the scales of justice? What happened to "innocent until proven guilty"? Sometimes people just don't realize what innocence means to innocent people. I've always believed in the justice system, but the justice system sleeps while James Dawson's family and friends remains awake. It's because the justice system sleeps that I have been blessed to be called to compile this documentary and use it as the roadmap to justice in my brother's death. Many of us find ourselves influenced by unfortunate situations beyond our control, but regardless of our situations, Jesus can empower us to become all he created us to be.

While the legal system insists on relegating the death of James Dawson to their files of statistics, the Lord refused to let

us fall by the wayside. How do we know when it's divine inter-
vention? When we know we could not have done it alone.

I thought after Ms. Renee Ferguson's story on March 7,
2001, our fight for justice would soon be ending. Jeraldine
Mosley-McCall, from Leak's staff, prepared James' body and
was shocked when she saw the empty cavity and said she did
not think James died by hanging because there should have
been bruising, contusions, or something. The pathologist, Dr.
James Bryant, saw the photographs of no marks on James'
neck, and he did not think that James died from hanging. The
mark on James' chin could have been anything under the sun,
but since all organs were taken, it was almost impossible for
another pathologist to examine the case. This should have been
more than enough for somebody to assist in our fight in this
wrongful death claim.

On March 14, 2001, I met with Mr. Eugene Pincham to discuss James' death. I gave him a copy of my fifty-page
documentary of incriminating evidence and the video tape of
the news story shown on March 7. We sat down for about an
hour, and I told him that our attorney had said they did not have
enough evidence to start an investigation. Mr. Pincham told me
that to have another attorney examine the case, we needed to be
released from our contract because no one could legally take
over the case if we didn't get a release. I was unaware of this. I
thought since our attorney told us they didn't have enough evidence to start an investigation, the contract voided itself.
Nevertheless, I went home and wrote a letter for Mom to sign,
releasing her contract from our attorney. After receiving the release, I mailed a copy to Mr. Pincham. Here is what he had to
say:

LAW OFFICES OF

COCHRAN, CHERRY, GIVENS SMITH & MONTGOMERY, L.L.C.

ONE NORTH LASALLE STREET • SUITE 2450
CHICAGO, ILLINOIS 60602
(312) 977-0200 • FAX: (312) 977-0209

March 21, 2001

Dear Ms. Dawson:

   I am in receipt of your letter which terminates our services as your attorney surrounding the death of your son, James Dawson. I pray that some day you will find answers to your many questions, and peace if your questions are never answered. I wish your family only the best, and I am sorry we could not help you.

   Again, thank you for considering our firm.

Very truly yours,

Douglas Hopson

DH:mr

4929 WILSHIRE BOULEVARD, SUITE 1010
LOS ANGELES, CALIFORNIA 90010

127 PEACHTREE STREET, NE
ATLANTA, GEORGIA 30303

WOOLWORTH BUILDING • 223 [
NEW YORK, NY 10279-0[

R. EUGENE PINCHAM
ATTORNEY AT LAW
9316 South Michigan Avenue
Chicago, Illinois 60619
#773/568-7927
#773/568-7938 Fax

April 11, 2001

The Dawson Family
c/o Margaret Dawson Brown

Re: James Dawson

Dear Dawson Family Members:

When I met with Margaret Dawson on March 14, 2001, I was unaware, and she did not inform me, that the matter of the death of James Dawson had been taken up with Attorney Douglas Hopson of the Cochran, Cherry, Givens, Smith & Montgomery law firm. You were kind enough to submit Attorney Hopson's letter dated March 21, 2001 to me. In view of the above and foregoing, I respectfully return the video and the articles regarding James Dawson that you submitted to me.

I am desperately trying to retire and it would be impossible for me to undertake the investigation that your request entails. I trust that you will be able to find another attorney who will be able to undertake your request. In the meantime, I will keep you uppermost in my prayers.

Stay well, and may the Good Lord continue to be with you and you with Him.

Sincerely,

R. Eugene Pincham

R. EUGENE PINCHAM
REP/cb
Encl.

Mr. Pincham's letter startled me because I sat in his office for an hour, and my entire conversation was about Attorney Hopson holding the case for four months then deciding there wasn't enough evidence to start an investigation. I guess it went over his head. I could not understand what difference it made who was holding the case. Mr. Pincham appeared a little alarmed when he realized the case was in the hands of the Cochran administration. Anyhow, may Mr. Pincham rest in peace.

Also, Attorney Hopson's letter struck me as a little off as well when he wrote, "I pray that some day you will find answers to your many questions, and peace if your questions are never answered." Maybe I'm just taking things too personally. I sent my fifty-page documentary to several other establishments, and here are their responses:

CHICAGO LAWYERS' COMMITTEE
FOR CIVIL RIGHTS UNDER LAW, INC.
100 NORTH LASALLE STREET ● SUITE 600 ● CHICAGO, ILLINOIS 60602-2403
(312) 630-9744 (Voice) ● (312) 630-9749 (TDD) ● (312) 630-1127 (Fax)

February 8, 2001

Mrs. Margaret Dawson Brown

Re: Your Letter Requesting Legal Assistance

Dear Ms. Brown:

We are in receipt of your letter requesting assistance and unfortunately, we are not able to provide you with representation. The work of the Chicago Lawyers' Committee is largely restricted to class action litigation addressing civil rights violations in employment, housing and mortgage & lending discrimination. It follows that your case is not one in which we would normally become involved. However, you may contact the Peoples Law Office at (773) 235-0070 and attorney Standish Willis at (312) 554-0005 to request their assistance.

I hope that our determination does not deter you from seeking assistance elsewhere. Good luck in your efforts to resolve your problem.

Sincerely,

Elesha Jackson
Office Manager

LAW OFFICE OF
STANDISH E. WILLIS
407 SOUTH DEARBORN STREET • SUITE 1395
CHICAGO, ILLINOIS 60605

TELEPHONE (312) 554-0005
FAX (312) 554-1012
E-MAIL swillis818@AOL.COM

June 14, 2001

Margaret Dawson Brown

Dear Ms Dawson Brown:

After review of your situation, we do not have the resources to handle the case to your potential wrongful death. We would like to involve the McCarthy Justice Center out of University of Chicago and with Attorney Locke Bowman, 1111 E. 60th Street, Chicago, IL 60637, telephone number (773)702-0349.

Thank you for considering the Law Office of Standish E. Willis. We have sent your information to him. We will be in touch with Locke Bowman for review. Please call him after Friday 15th 2001.

Very Truly yours,

DEMITRUS EVANS

June 25, 2001

Margaret (Dawson) Brown

Dear Ms. Brown:

Thank you for contacting the American Civil Liberties Union of Illinois. We have carefully reviewed your situation, and we regret to inform you that we will not be able to accept your case.

Generally, the ACLU challenges governmental action that poses a threat to the civil liberties or civil rights of a group of persons. We also accept some individual cases where a favorable decision will extend civil rights protection to a broad class of people.

The fact that we cannot help you does not mean that your case has no merit. It may be that we are handling a similar case, that the case does not involve a novel issue pertaining to civil liberties, or that we do not have the resources to handle the case.

With regard to your dissatisfaction with the legal assistance you have been able to obtain, you may want to contact Attorney Registration and Disciplinary Commission of the Supreme Court of Illinois at 130 E. Randolph Plaza, Chicago, IL 60601-6219. The phone number is 312-826-8625.

You should be aware that there is a limited time in which legal action may be pursued, sometimes referred to as a statute of limitations. You should contact an attorney for advice about preserving any rights that you may have.

Please accept our regrets that we cannot assist you with your problem.

Sincerely,

Ruth Belfer
Intake Office

167

July 6, 2001

Standish E. Willis
407 S. Dearborn, Suite 1395
Chicago, Illinois 60605

Dear Stan:

Thanks for sending me the materials on James Dawson's potential case. It is a very sad situation, but we're not in a position to help with it.

Sincerely,

Locke E. Bowman

I met with Mr. Furmin Sessoms from the NAACP south-side branch office on the same day I met with Mr. Pincham. I called the office to make an appointment, and it took two weeks to get an appointment. When I arrived for the appointment, I was in the office no longer than ten minutes. I began to discuss the unusual circumstances surrounding my brother's death, but when I told Mr. Sessoms I had just met with Mr. Eugene Pincham, he stopped me and told me to call him when I heard back from Mr. Pincham. I was in shock. I could not believe that his decision to listen to what I had to say depended solely on what Mr. Pincham was going to do. That is when I realized if it were not a high-profile case constantly in the media, most civil rights organizations and legal representatives will not jump on the bandwagon.

I tried to make an appointment to meet with Rev. Jesse Jackson of the Rainbow Push Coalition. Several members of his congregation attended James' funeral, and Mr. Propter even videotaped it. Unfortunately, it was while Mr. Jackson was receiving a bit of media scrutiny in his own affairs, so I was unable to meet with him. However, I met with Mr. Mark Allen, field director of the Rainbow Push Coalition. I talked with Mr. Allen for almost two hours. During the meeting, he showed me stacks of letters from individuals that had written in search of justice for loved ones found hanging in jail. I was stunned. I had assumed my brother was an isolated incident, but once I appeared on WVON and met with Mr. Allen, I realized it was an epidemic, as common as a cold. When I told Mr. Allen where the hanging occurred, he told me it happened all the time in rural areas. I asked why it continued to happen, and why nobody did anything about it. He could not answer me. I left Mr. Allen thinking that since no one could do anything about it, at least I could let people know about it.

Remember the story of Ron Settles, who was stopped for speeding in 1983; he also ended up dead, found hanging while detained in jail. The coroner ruled his injuries consistent with a suicide.

NATIONAL REPORT

Ron Settles Case (1983): Cochran reached a $760,000 settlement in the case of Ron Settles, a Cal State Long Beach football star who was stopped for speeding in the Southern California town of Signal Hill. He reportedly "refused to cooperate" with officers during the stop and was later arrested. He was taken to police headquarters and put into a cell. Three hours later he was found dead, hanging from the cell bars. The coroner ruled his injuries were consistent with suicide. A jury found it was not a suicide, but a homicide, and the town settled the $50 million civil suit. The payment was the most that had ever been paid in California in a police abuse case. "And the money talked loudly,"

Cochran said. "To make sure that city would never again be faced with that kind of situation, the people of Signal Hill voted a reform government into city hall, the police chief was replaced, and the police department was reorganized."

This is one of the rare stories that turned victim into victory. Thank God for Attorney Cochran and all the success he has had in his career. I tried to speak with Mr. Cochran to let him know the unusual circumstances surrounding James' death, but I could only speak to the associates. I was told that since the case was already in the hands of an attorney from their law firm, we had to deal directly with him. In other words, there was no getting around Mr. Hopson. I truly believe that if this had been a high-profile case, I would have been able to speak with Mr. Cochran. May Mr. Cochran rest in peace.

There were other radio stations and television programs I wanted to contact however, I realized there was only so much I could talk about in the amount of time that would be given. Even in my fifty-page documentary, there was only so much I could talk about. This documentary, As I travel through the valley of death, allowed me to let it all out. I know I may have overlooked some things of importance, but I think I covered just about everything possible for a sister.

It wasn't until after Ms. Ferguson's story on March 7 that I opened the re-autopsy report. I was so focused on all the other evidence I was compiling that I simply overlooked reading it. After the independent pathologist on November 9, 2000, confirmed that strangulation was the cause of death and that James' body was an empty cavity when they re-opened it, I could not see what they could examine with no organs and no blood to prove cause of death. When I opened the re-autopsy report and read the introductory letter, I was shocked. It was simply unbelievable. The letter was nothing like the concerned phone call on November 9.

It stated, "In summary, your son died from asphyxiation secondary to hanging by apparent suicidal intent while being in detention by the Illinois State Police Department. The postmortem examination did not reveal any signs of a struggle or violence prior to death, or suggest that the asphyxiation by hanging was anything other than by suicidal intent. The autopsy report from the initial postmortem examination performed by the Springfield Medical Examiner's office, as well as blood and urine tests for common drugs of abuse performed during the first postmortem examination have not been received by the time of completion of this autopsy."

I realize the body was identified with an I.D. tag attached to the toe, but I did not realize James' detention status with the Illinois State Police Department was attached to the toe as well. I paid $975 for an independent conclusion, not confirmation with the Springfield medical examiner's office. How can it be professionally said, "The asphyxiation by hanging was anything other than by suicidal intent?" Was the independent pathologist inside the jail cell with James? Was he aware of all the suspicious circumstances surrounding James' death? Did he know that none of the individuals initially involved with James' body could identify any marks on his neck? Did he know that James Dawson's family photographed the neck immediately after he was pronounced dead to show no marks on his neck?

The re-autopsy report stated, "The external examination reveals an oblique 5.1 cm long strangulation mark on the right side of the neck, under the chin." The final pathologic diagnosis stated, "Oblique strangulation mark on the upper lateral portion of the neck." 5.1 cm. long equals about 2 inches. Since the mark is described on the right side, this has to be the exact same mark every individual initially involved with James body has described being on the chin. The independent pathologist has left us to ask, is the upper lateral portion of the neck considered the chin?

Let's rewind to the initial descriptions for a moment. The code blue report stated, initial skin condition, 2 inch abrasion on the chin, underneath the chin. The Springfield pathologist report stated, a mark beneath the chin was secondary to the pressure of the bed sheet. The investigating officer report stated there is a mark on the chin, underneath the chin that was earlier at the hospital and possibly by some of the emergency medical people reported as an abrasion. The coroner report stated, there is a notation of a mark made by the bed sheet beneath the chin. Again, not one time do any of these individuals identify with a mark being on James neck. I tried contacting the independent pathologist for over three months requesting a copy of the photograph they must have of the mark they document on James' neck, underneath the chin, but I received no response. Here is the copy of the re-autopsy report:

MICHAEL W. KAUFMAN, M. D., LTD.

DEPARTMENT OF PATHOLOGY

EVANSTON HOSPITAL

2650 RIDGE AVENUE

EVANSTON, ILLINOIS 60201-1782

———

(847) 570-2753

FAX (847) 570-2927

December 18, 2000

Re: James Dawson/Autopsy #EHA00-173

Dear Mrs. Dawson:

Enclosed please find the completed final autopsy report on your son, James Dawson, whose re-autopsy we performed at Evanston Hospital on November 9, 2000, autopsy number EHA00-173.

In summary, your son died from asphyxiation secondary to hanging by apparent suicidal intent while he was in detention by the Illinois State Police Department. The postmortem examination did not reveal any evidence of a struggle or violence prior to his death, or to suggest that the asphyxiation by hanging was anything other than by suicidal intent. The autopsy report of the initial postmortem examination performed by the Springfield County Medical Examiner's Office, as well as blood and urine tests for common drugs of abuse performed during the first postmortem examination have not been received by the time of completion of this autopsy report.

If you, or any other member of your family, have any questions about this autopsy report, please do not hesitate to contact either one of us at the above telephone number.

Sincerely,

Michael W. Kaufman

Michael W. Kaufman, MD

Eugene Kouzov

Eugene Kouzov, MD

EVANSTON NORTHWESTERN HEALTHCARE

EVANSTON HOSPITAL	GLENBROOK HOSPITAL	HIGHLAND PARK HOSPITAL
2650 Ridge Avenue	2100 Pfingsten Road	718 Glenview Avenue
Evanston, IL 60201	Glenview, IL 60025	Highland Park, IL 60035
Ph. (847) 570-2748	Ph. (847) 657-5688	Ph. (847) 480-3755

REPORT OF AUTOPSY

Patient: **DAWSON, JAMES** Autopsy #: **EHA-00-00173**
Autopsy By: KOUZOV/KAUFMAN SS#: ~S2

EXTERNAL EXAMINATION:

The body is identified as James Dawson by the attached right great toe ID tag. The body is that of an adult African-American male who appears approximately the stated age of 37 years. The body measures approximately 170 cm in length and weighs approximately 85 kilograms. There is moderate rigor mortis of the upper and lower extremities and of the jaws and mild livor mortis. The body is cold to the touch. The skin is darkly pigmented and is without jaundice. The body has been previously autopsied. The scalp hair is shaved. The facial features are symmetrical and no scars or abrasions of the face are identified. The sclerae are a mottled white with petechial hemorrhages of the conjunctivae identified. The irides are brown and the pupils measure 0.3 cm in diameter, bilaterally. The nose and ears are each grossly unremarkable with no evidence of prior hemorrhage or drainage. The dentition is preserved. The anterior teeth, lips, and gums are each grossly unremarkable, with no evidence of trauma, laceration or other gross abnormalities. The oropharynx is inaccessible due to rigor mortis of the jaws. The mucosa lining the tongue is dry but is without lacerations or abrasions. The neck is normally shaped. Examination reveals an oblique 5.1 cm long strangulation mark located on the right side of the neck under the chin. The neck organs have not been previously removed. The hyoid bone is intact with no palpable fractures or dislocations. The subcutaneous soft tissues of the right upper portion of the lateral neck demonstrate minimal hemorrhage within the area of the strangulation mark. An incision is performed on the back side of the neck. There are no hemorrhages, signs of contusion or broken cervical vertebrae identified on examination. The thorax has a normal contour and contains a recently sutured Y-shaped incision consistent with a prior postmortem examination. The left and right arms of the Y-shaped incision measure 25.0 and 27.0 cm in length, respectively. The breasts are male type and are normally developed. There are no scars or gross abnormalities of the chest identified. The abdomen is flat. A postmortem sutured vertical midline incision which measures 30.0 cm in length is present and is consistent with prior postmortem examination. There are no scars, ecchymoses, abrasions or other axillary or cervical lymphadenopathy is palpable. The upper and lower extremities are symmetric. The skin of the upper extremities is smooth and unremarkable. No scars, lacerations or abrasions are identified. Longitudinal incision are performed on both wrists, and the subcutaneous tissue do no show any sign of hemorrhage or trauma. The skin of the lower extremities is without lacerations, abrasion or trauma. No cyanosis of the fingernail beds or other gross abnormalities of the extremities are identified. Examination of the back reveals no evidence of ecchymoses, abrasions or other gross abnormalities.

BODY CAVITIES:

The prior Y-shaped incision is reopened. The detached chest plate is examined and no fractures or hemorrhages of the sternum or ribcage are identified. The thoracic, abdominal and cranial cavities are empty. There is no specimen bag with organs identified. The cranial, thoracic and abdominal cavities are grossly free of abnormalities.

Director of Laboratory: Thomas Victor, M.D., Ph.D.

NECK ORGANS:
The larynx, proximal half of the trachea and the attached thyroid gland and adjacent tongue are removed en bloc. Several longitudinal incisions of the tongue are placed and they show normal homogeneous light brown skeletal muscle. There are no areas of hemorrhage or submucosal trauma identified. The mucosa of the larynx and of the trachea is light tan. Small spots of brownish discoloration measuring between 0.2 and 0.4 cm in diameter are seen on the mucosa of the right lateral aspect of the larynx. The proximal half of the esophagus contains a normal light tan unremarkable mucosa. The thyroid gland weighs 21.0 grams. Cut sectioning reveals a light brown unremarkable parenchyma. The parathyroid glands are not grossly identified. Several longitudinal incisions are placed in the musculature lateral to the trachea. The soft tissues are light brown without hemorrhages or trauma. Cut sectioning of the soft tissues of the upper neck reveals lobulated submandibular glands measuring between 2.0 and 3.5 cm in greatest dimension. Cut sectioning reveals an unremarkable light tan parenchyma.

MICROSCOPIC EXAMINATION:
SECTIONS:
1   Tongue, anterior portion
2   Tongue, posterior portion
3   Larynx with mucosal congestion
4   Trachea
5   Thyroid gland
6   Esophagus
7   Epiglottis
8   Soft tissues, right side of neck
9   Submandibular salivary gland

TONGUE:
Histologic sections from the anterior and posterior portions of the tongue (blocks 1 & 2) show a keratinized squamous epithelium overlying striated muscle which is microscopically unremarkable. There are no abrasions, lacerations, or any sign of physical trauma.

LARYNX:
Histologic sections from the area of mucosal congestion of the right lateral wall of the larynx (block 3) demonstrate submucosal vascular and soft tissue congestion. The overlying mucosa is ciliated and normal-appearing. These histologic changes can be attributed to stagnation of blood flow due to the asphyxiation. There is a moderate degree of submucosal vascular dilatation and congestion. In addition, the submucosa demonstrates a moderate degree of chronic inflammation. The overlying mucosa is preserved

THYROID GLAND:
The thyroid gland demonstrates a moderate degree of vascular congestion.

ESOPHAGUS:
No pathologic abnormalities are observed on histologic examination.

EPIGLOTTIS:
There is a moderate degree of submucosal vascular dilatation and congestion.

SUBMANDIBULAR GLAND AND NECK SOFT TISSUES:
Histologic sections from the submandibular gland demonstrate preserved, mostly serous, acini. The sections from the neck soft tissues demonstrate normal-appearing striated muscle.

CLINICAL-PATHOLOGIC CORRELATION:
The patient, Mr. James Dawson, was a 37-year-old African-American male with no known significant past medical history. The patient was being detained by the Illinois State Police Department on November 6, 2000 when he was found hanging in his detention cell. An initial autopsy was performed by the Springfield County Medical Examiner's Office in Springfield, IL.

Director of Laboratory: Thomas Victor, M.D., Ph.D.

EVANSTON HOSPITAL
2650 Ridge Avenue
Evanston, IL 60201
Ph. (847) 570-2748

GLENBROOK HOSPITAL
2100 Pfingsten Road
Glenview, IL 60025
Ph. (647) 667-5688

HIGHLAND PARK HOSPITAL
718 Glenview Avenue
Highland Park, IL 60035
Ph. (847) 480-3755

REPORT OF AUTOPSY

Patient: **DAWSON, JAMES**
Sex: M   Age: 37
HH#:
SS#:   DOB: 7/7/63
Zip: B
            Occ: N/A

Autopsy #: **EHA-00-00173**
Date of Admission: N/A
DEATH - Date: 11/06/2000
Time: UNKNOWN
AUTOPSY - Date: 11/09/2000
Time:

Physician: ASSIGNED PHYSICIANS-NO,   Autopsy By: KOUZOV/KAUFMAN
Restrictions: NONE

FINAL PATHOLOGIC DIAGNOSIS

1. Asphyxiation secondary to hanging by apparent suicidal intent while in custody during detention by the Illinois State Police department with:
   a. oblique strangulation mark of the right upper lateral portion of the neck (5.1 cm in length and 1.5 cm in width)
   b. submucosal congestion of the right lateral wall of the larynx, thyroid gland and trachea
   c. petechial hemorrhge of the conjunctivae
   d. lack of evidence of physical struggle

Immediate cause of death:

Asphyxiation secondary to hanging by apparent suicidal intent

Main disease:

None

Eugene Kouzov/MK
EUGENE KOUZOV, MD
EK/MK/bjk
12/18/2000

Michael Kaufman
MICHAEL KAUFMAN, MD
12/18/00
DATE OF SIGNATURE

Director of Laboratory: Thomas Victor, M.D., Ph.D.

Dead bodies are not supposed to bruise. Studies show that abrasions and contusions received at the time of death cannot be readily told from those received after death, but abrasions occurring after death have a different appearance than pre-postmortem abrasions. A pathologist is supposed to be able to tell the difference. Rigor mortis refers to the progressive stiffening of muscles that occurs several hours after death because of coagulation of muscle protein. To *coagulate* is to cause a liquid to become a soft, semisolid mass.

Studies show there can be no strangulation without a strangulation mark—smothering or suffocating, perhaps, but not strangulation. Smothering occurs when an obstructing object, such as a pillow or blanket, closes the airways. If a soft object is used, the body will show no visible signs of trauma. Hanging done with a bed sheet will leave a soft ligature on the neck. It will leave abrasions and compression marks characterized by multiple, irregular patterns that reflect the shape of a bunched cloth. Hangings done with other objects, such as a rope, electrical cord, or a belt will leave an inverted V-shape bruise, and are easily told from ligature strangulation (murder), which leaves a straight-line bruise.

Studies show the most difficult cause of death to determine from a medical examiner's point of view is strangulation or suffocation because these two causes may not leave marks outside the body. In "asphyxia," because of the lack of oxygen getting to the body, and with poisoning as well, there may be no clues on the outside of the body indicating an unnatural death, let alone a homicide. So these causes require the most careful of dissections, particularly the neck organs. According to the re-autopsy report, James' neck organs were untouched. Anyway, it is important to look under the skin of the neck for small signs of trauma—usually hemorrhage, sometimes fracture—because they can easily be missed.

Hanging produces death by strangulation (asphyxia) due to the weight of the person's body pulling down on the noose, causing it to tighten, constricting the trachea (air passage), and applying pressure to the large blood vessels in the neck. The condemned usually struggles for some time due to the pain caused by the noose. It takes several minutes for a person to lapse into unconsciousness. Strangulation by ligature may be homicidal or suicidal. Close inspection of the marks left on the skin may show the type of garrote used. Differentiating between hanging and strangulation is an age-old problem, and much depends on the investigating officer. A careful study of the ligature material and the ligature mark and their comparative, makes it possible to conclude if a case of strangulation was fabricated as a hanging.

Because "suicide" was the official cause of death, Mom was denied payments from James' life insurance policies, to which she was the beneficiary. Most life insurance policies do not honor suicides. Families are left with the financial burden of the funeral and burial. Here is the correspondence with Met Life:

Johnstown Client Relations Center
500 Schoolhouse Road, Johnstown, PA 15904-2914

MetLife®

LILLIE DAWSON

Re: Policy: 853 017 594 UL
        Measuring Life: James Dawson

Dear Mrs Dawson,

This acknowledges receipt of your correspondence. Please accept our condolences on the loss of your son.

We have reviewed your request for payment of the Settlement Death Benefit amount in relation to the above policy. As described in the MetLife Class Action Benefit voucher, a Settlement Death Benefit is payable, during the coverage period, upon the death of the person known as the Measuring Life (excluding death resulting from suicide, while sane or insane). The Measuring Life for policy 853017594 UL was James Dawson.

Based on the cause of death as listed on the death certificate submitted for our review, the Settlement Death Benefit in relation to this policy is not payable.

If you have any questions or if any additional information is needed, please feel free to contact us at the address listed on this letter or by calling 877-474-0389.

Sincerely,

Kimberly M. Katrancha
General Relief Administration

June 19, 2001

178

Johnstown Client Relations Center
500 Schoolhouse Road Johnstown PA 15904

MetLife®

LILLIE DAWSON

Re: Policy: 853 107 594 UL
James Dawson

Dear Ms.Dawson

This acknowledges receipt of your recent correspondence and will supplement our prior letter.

Once the circumstances surrounding your son's death have been determined, we would be willing to review copies of any official documentation that you can provide. In the event an amended death certificate is issued, a copy will be needed for our files.

If you have any questions or if any additional information is needed, please feel free to contact us at the address listed on this letter or by calling 877-474-0389.

Sincerely

Chris Boring

Chris Boring
General Relief Administration

August 31, 2001

Metropolitan Life Insurance Company

Two years into my investigation, no wind of legal assistance has blown our way. It is unfortunate that justice doesn't come automatically or freely, and that we have to fight for it. If this had been a high-profile case constantly in the media, I guarantee we would not have had to worry about looking for legal assistance; legal assistance would have been knocking our door down. If I could have filed the wrongful death claim myself, I would have. I know it is one thing to file a claim. That claim needs to be presented beyond a reasonable doubt, although I feel our claim is. Never in my wildest dreams could I have ever imagined that I would be writing a book about my brother's life and death; this was never my intention. My intention was to gather as much incriminating evidence as I could, pass it on to our attorney, and let him do what he did best—investigate. Attorneys are aware of the legal ramifications. That is their job, their profession. I am a distribution clerk for the United States Postal Service. I just assumed since our wrongful death claim was in the best hands possible, with the Cochran administration, that my family had absolutely nothing to worry about; the case should be a slam-dunk. Since it was not, I had to step completely out of my comfort zone, into a field of well-educated, professional individuals with prestigious positions, and challenge them.

I was employed with the postal service for the past twenty-three years. I received numerous awards and recognition for my speed and accuracy in the distribution of the mail. I went over and beyond the call of duty whenever I was on the clock—even when I wasn't. My job was my livelihood, and I loved my job. Everything I had revolved around my job. My life insurance, medical insurance, not just for me, but for my grandchildren as well. My savings plan, retirement plan—everything revolved around my job.

Two years after my brother's death I continued to go to work every night. I worked the night shift throughout my career. I was a changed person in those two years. Things I used to laugh at were no longer funny. Things I used to take with a grain of salt, I now took deep to the core. I was more serious than I had ever been. With two full-time jobs, working my brother's cold case, some nights when it came time for me to go to work, I was so exhausted I would call in. The more incriminating evidence I uncovered and the more I was ignored by the legal system, the more I felt victimized and that my family's rights were being violated in every way imaginable. Realizing my personal investigation was interfering with my attendance, I requested an indefinite leave of absence. I was denied. My immediate supervisors told me that I needed to stop my personal investigation. If Cochran's people couldn't do anything about it, what made me think I could? I wasn't a lawyer. I was told people died everyday in wrongful deaths, so what made my brother's death so special, and what made me think people wanted to read what I was writing about? The criticism and aggravation from some of the managers was worse than my brother's death. I truly understood what "going postal" really meant.

I wrote a letter to the postmaster disclosing the aggravation I was receiving from some of the managers and requested he grant me an indefinite leave of absence. The postmaster granted me a thirty-day leave of absence, not nearly enough time to do what I had to do. After I returned from the thirty days, I requested additional time off and was denied. I asked to speak with someone from the Employee's Assistance Program (E.A.P). Unfortunately, it took seventeen months for me to receive an appointment. Why it took so long is beyond my comprehension. I was told it took so long because I got off work at 6:30 and the office did not open until 8:30. Of course, I didn't believe that. I went the appointment seventeen months later, but there was nothing they could do for me by then. I had already gone through too much. After I met the E.A.P representative on May 21, 2002, the aggravation continued. Three months later, on August 24, 2002, I resigned.

I did receive plenty of support from my co-workers and most of the managers, but unfortunately, the aggravation I was receiving was from my immediate supervisors, and I had to deal

with them every night. I even put in a request to change supervisors, but I was denied. Not everybody is going to support you,
no matter what kind of hardship you are going through. The
world is not going to stop just because you have problems. I
took the criticism to heart because I knew there were many who
felt as my supervisors did—only they did not have the heart to
say it to my face. So I appreciated the criticism, but not the aggravation. It could only make me or break me, and I refused to
let it break me.

A year after leaving the postal service, my immediate supervisor died and the others received even worst tragedies in the
deaths of their loved ones. I was at the funerals lending my support and giving my condolences to them and their families in
their time of bereavement. You just never know what tragedy
lies around the corner. The position I held for twenty-three
years no longer existed. The postal service, like many indus-
tries, has turned to modern technology; computers now
distribute the bulk of the mail. My decision to resign was the
ultimate sacrifice. With the competitiveness of college graduates and having no degree to fall back on—oh, yeah, I made the
ultimate sacrifice. With the economy in bad shape and recession
hitting harder than ever, and so many people loosing their jobs,
oh yeah, I made the ultimate sacrifice. I received a check for
$50,000 when I resigned, but I used to make $75,000 to
$80,000 a year with overtime. The $50,000 had to last me until I
decided to do whatever I was going to do. By resigning, I for-
feited unemployment and state or federal assistance, so I had to
make the best of my situation. A year after my resignation, we
still had not received any legal assistance. I became so depressed I stopped writing for almost two years. As everyone
continued to go on with their lives, I was frozen in time on the
day that my brother died. I could not flash forward to the future
without closure of that day. My family and friends wanted me
to give up my fight because they saw that it was becoming very
difficult for me. Lord forbid if any sickness was to come my

way and I had to go to the doctor. With no medical insurance, I would have to pay out of pocket. If I die before completing this documentary, somebody will have to pay for my funeral, so I continue to pray for good health and to one day look justice in the face. I remain optimistic because I know that I have more fight left in me. I know God did not bring me this far to turn back now. I cannot dwell on those forces of darkness because then I am tying the hands of almighty God. I refuse to accept mediocrity. I must continue to cast out negative thoughts and recognize God is working in my life. I may not see any progress of getting my story out to the world right now, but that does not mean that God is not working in my life. It says in Philippians 2:13, God is constantly at work in those who believe.

I can never give up my fight for justice, no matter what I have to go through. I want to turn my victim mentality into victory by completing this documentary and presenting it to the world. When I started back writing, it was if I had never stopped. Everything came back as if it had just happened. I never thought my investigation would put me in the position to quit my job and lose everything to bring the story of my brother's death to life. November 6, 2009, will mark the ninth-year anniversary of his death, and I have given all I have to give. Fighting for justice should not have had to come at such an enormous price. Now it is time for me to let go of my story and exhale. You may now review the letter from the postmaster, followed by the letter from the E.A.P representative.

Sr., PLANT MANAGER
CHICAGO CARDISS COLLINS PROCESSING AND DISTRIBUTION CENTER

UNITED STATES
POSTAL SERVICE

December 6, 2001

Dear Ms. Brown

This is in response to your letter requesting an indefinite leave of absence due to circumstances regarding the death of your brother.

I will grant you a detail for 30 days, which would give you the opportunity to continue the investigation into the death of your brother.

Please accept my personal apology for any aggravation you experienced from tour one management.

Sincerely,

Patrick L. Farrell

/mms:9997

cc: Akinyinka O. Akinyele
     Lewis Woodall
     Donna M. Young

433 W. HARRISON ST RM 7032
CHICAGO IL 60607-9997
(312) 983-7519
FAX: (312) 983-7696

EMPLOYEE ASSISTANCE PROGRAM

CONFIDENTIAL

June 4, 2002

Margaret Brown

Dear Margaret,

Recently, you participated in services provided by the Employee Assistance Program (EAP) but declined another follow up appointment during the intake interview of 5/21/2002.

Is there any further service that the EAP can offer you? If so, please call me at the number below. If we do not hear from you within the next two weeks, we will assume that you do not wish services at this time.

Your case will be closed and Client Satisfaction Survey will be sent to you. Your comments will help us to improve the quality of services that the EAP provides to you and to other employees.

Thank you for your participation and assistance.

Sincerely,

Barbara Hunter, LCSW
Federal Occupational Health EAP Counselor
312-983-8604 local office
(800) 327-4968 national 24 hours

Federal Occupational Health (FOH)   Employee Assistance Program (EAP)

My Testimony

After every legal route I took hit a major roadblock and no one was able to assist in my fight for justice, I had to disconnect my mind from my brother's death and connect my mind to God. I had to go outside my limitations, and by faith, move into the unsearchable riches of Christ. When we have a vision, God is able to take us outside our mental ability, access our situation, and send us on a mission. When God calls us out, he does not tell us where we are going or give us directions on how to get there. God is able to just root us up from whatever it is that we are doing. I actually thought I had called on God, but he had called on me. If it were up to me to have a vision of traveling through the valley of my brother's death, I could not have tackled this journey. God called me and James' death rooted me up from everything that was part of my life. We tend to become content in whatever we are doing. We just get caught up in our ways, but the call from God is very powerful, and once we've come in contact with him, we will never be the same.

It is a true statement that experience is the best teacher. I must say I have truly learned we may be dealt serious cards in our lives. When we play the Lord as the highest card in our decks, we cannot go wrong. We may sometimes feel the Lord does not come when we want him to, but my testimony is that he is always on time. If we knew what card life was about to deal us, we would not need God. We would already have direction to our lives and know exactly what lay ahead. We could just meet God there. But since we don't, we need to walk with God. God called me out to direct me to where he wanted me to go, and he did not send me alone. He sent me on a mission of hope, a quest for justice, and a journey into an untouched world. There comes a time when we can't see our way, but we don't have to when we know God is with us. We are all God's private collections.

...If we are still crying, God is not through with us yet!

...If we are still hurting, God is not through with us yet!

...If we are still suffering, God is not through with us yet!

Accepting the Lord as the head of our lives and learning all we can about what he has to offer is much more than this world could ever offer. Why not take time out of our busy schedules to find out what is going on with that higher power? We will be the sole beneficiaries of this investigation, and this is one investigation we don't have to stay clear of. Unfortunately, no one can give or loan us the benefit of experiencing the greatness of the Lord. We are in that event all by ourselves. The choice is ours, the rewards are plentiful, and it won't cost us a thing. To receive the assurance that we will have eternal life is indeed a blessing, and we all have the same choice, so take it. There's an open book, a letter from Christ, and our own personal testimonies will be enough.

...When God wakes us up in the middle of our situation, takes us to a place to believe the unbelievable and gives us a vision!

...When God takes us outside of our comprehension, outside of our intellect, outside of our capacity, and outside the perimeter of our knowledge!

...When God takes us outside our minds, moves us into the Christian and spiritual arenas of the exceeding greatness of his powers and widens our horizons!

...When God makes a statement and starts working with us. Let there be no mistake that once God is done working with us, we will know that it had to be God. Nobody can take the credit but God.

We generally depend on our own abilities and the abilities of others. We generally depend on being able to see where we are going by relying on our own safe grounds. What we are doing is limiting the operations of God. When I came to the end of all I could do, searching and hoping for justice in my brother's death, God provided an understanding of his will and his promises. God is with us always, but we have to work with him. In quietness and confidence, this shall be our strength. Keep in mind these three very important steps:

...With God's help, I am doing this!

...With God's help, I can do this!

...God and I have done it!

If we believe this, if we practice this, if we just yield ourselves to this, it does not matter what obstacles or difficulties we face; the Lord is with us always. To be lost, only to be found. The Lord is the higher power that can make a way out of no way; such is the hope of his calling me out with an expectation. He can pick us up and never lets us down, leaving only his footprints as we look back, because his powers are exhaustless!

Closing Arguments

Ladies and gentlemen, you have been introduced to the life and death of James Dawson. It took me nine years to compile and write this documentary. I thought I would never finish. Although there are statutes of limitations for filing a wrongful death claim, there are no statutes of limitations for murder. The incriminating evidence I place before you are not just my words, but words of powerful individuals, specialists in their fields, individuals whose words are considered law.

We have the jail staff, who of course, will never admit any wrongdoing. We have the Toledo emergency medical team, the paramedics, who can only go with what has been presented to them by the jail staff. Who, I ask, is going to go against what the jail staff said happened? If it is proven that James' death did not occur the way the jail staff said it did, and there are those involved in any type of cover-up, it will bring a lot of attention to the wrongful death claim for James Dawson.

The paramedics are neighbors of the jail, and they do not want to challenge what the jail staff said happened. It was their town, and they did not need any wrongdoing slapped in their faces. Well, we, the family and friends of James Dawson, feel the same way. We do not want a false suicide label slapped in our faces; therefore, we are all on the same page. What makes their position so much stronger is who they are and the powerful positions they hold.

So, in the moment when the family of James Dawson arrives inside the jail, they must suddenly set the stage and bring to life the most problem-free route to the most difficult cause of death to prove—a suicide hanging. The jail staff said that the bed sheet (mattress cover) was tied around the shower curtain rod then around James' neck. His feet were resting on the floor and he could have stood up to prevent his death. The cell James occupied—let's talk about this cell one last time. The cell consisted of a bunk, a sink, a toilet, a shower with a shower rod and no shower curtain, a pay telephone, and an outside exit, another entrance to the cell. This is some kind of cell. I bet this is the only cell inside the entire jail like this.

The hanging allegedly took place between 11:20 and 11:50. Now, when James was escorted back to the cell after talking to Mom at 2:17 a.m., what was there for him to do but lie down and sleep until his family arrives? It might have been difficult going to sleep knowing there was another entrance to the cell. Nevertheless, according to the jail staff, James was alive until 11:20. The trustee who they claimed fed James breakfast at 7:30 never stated whether James was awake or acknowledged the trustee. He never said whether James ate the breakfast. James was very particular about his food. He knew his family was on their way, so if he was alive, he may have perhaps drunk water or juice, but to have eaten their food? I don't think so. He would have just waited for Mom's cooking or have gone somewhere to eat. Since James' body was completely cleaned out, we will never know what food was in the digestive system, or if poison was indeed a factor.

The scene was set. The same trustee who fed James breakfast at 7:30 witnessed him lying down at 11:05. Correctional Officer Cornell again witnessed him lying down at 11:20. Bail was paid ten minutes after Officer Cornell saw James lying down. It took Officer Cornell twenty minutes to arrive at James' cell after bail was paid. Why did it take her so long to get to the cell? Only she knows the answer to that. Conveniently, in those twenty minutes, James got up from the bunk and decided to hang himself after staying alive for over nine hours. Officer Cornell said that when she arrived at the cell, James was partially hanging and could have stood up. She couldn't understand this. Believe me, she understood. She might not have wanted to understand, but she understood. I do not think James ever got up from the bunk after Officer Cornell saw him lying down at

11:20. I think James was dead long before Officer Cornell arrived at his cell twenty minutes after bail was paid. There is no way James' hand would have been "ice cold" when Mom touched him. It takes a while for the body temperature to drop. There was not enough time for him to have turned that cold.

What really hurts so much about this entire allegation is that the trip from Chicago to the jail is three hours, and the weather conditions delayed my family's arrival half an hour. If my family had not been delayed, they would have arrived at the jail around 11:00. According to the jail staff, James was alive until 11:20. We wouldn't even be going through this. Can you imagine how heavy this must weigh on a family, knowing that twenty minutes made a difference between life and death?

Officer Cornell said the bed sheet was tied around the shower rod then around James' neck. When the Toledo emergency medical team arrived, the jail staff had already taken down the body. They were the only ones to witness the hanging. If the hanging occurred between the hours of 11:20 and 11:50, within a thirty-minute period, and the bed sheet was tied around James' neck even with James' feet resting on the floor, the bed sheet impression only left a mark on the right side of the chin, underneath the chin. The independent pathologist put it on the "upper lateral portion of the neck." The bed sheet left no marks on the front of the neck, no marks on the back of the neck, and no marks on the left side of the neck, only on the right side. That is incredible.

When the ambulance arrived at the hospital, we had two different versions of events. Of course, I am going to go with my family's version because, as I have stated, they sat in their vehicle waiting on James to be released, watching that clock. Their time frame, plus the actions recorded in the Code Blue report, plus the actions documented in the emergency room, plus the time the Code Blue notes mention Dr. Czelatdko corroborates my family's recollection. There is no way, according to the risk manager's version, that James arrived at the hospital at 12:31, dead on arrival, and they started working on him six minutes later. They worked on him for an entire twenty-eight minutes then pronounced him dead on arrival, and during those twenty-eight minutes, there was no pulse and no blood pressure. James was dead long before he was pronounced dead. The cardiac life support reading (electrocardiogram) taken from James' medical records. The time runs from 12:37 until 1:04, the exact same time recorded on the Code Blue record, and the exact same time the family followed the ambulance to the hospital.

When I compared the electrocardiogram reading to the Code Blue record to the Sarah Bush Lincoln Health Center bill, this is what I uncovered. If a paramedic or physician were to look at these documents, they could tell us exactly what everything meant. However, this is not my profession, I'm just traveling through the valley of death.

At 12:37, the starting time on the Code Blue record it stated, "No blood pressure/ no pulse, and cardiac rhythm asystole." Asystole is a state in which the heart is not beating and has no electrical activity. There is no cardiac output. Asystole is incompatible with life. Untreated for more than a couple of minutes, it will result in irreversible brain damage, then death. Although the appearance of asystole on an electrocardiogram is known colloquially as a flat line, a completely flat line is uncommon as an ECG trace. Pulseless electrical activity, as the name states, is a rhythm abnormality in which there is electrical activity from the heart but no pump function, and therefore no pulse or blood pressure.

At 12:39, the Code Blue record stated, "Medications Epi 10,000 IVP." Epi is epinephrine, which is used to treat cardiac arrest. It narrows the blood vessels and opens airways to the lungs.

At 12:42, the Code Blue record stated, "Cardiac rhythm is at ventricular fibrillation." Defib joules are shocks. James was shocked six times, from 12:42 until 12:53.

At 12:45 the Code Blue record stated, "Epi 10,000 IVP was administered and at 12:51, and 12:59."

At 12:53 which is the same time the code blue introduced the emergency room physician, 300 mg. of Cardarone was administer. Cardarone is an antarrhythmic used to treat an irregular heartbeat and maintain a normal heart rate.

I am trying to separate the paramedics' actions from the hospital's actions, since we have two separate periods of twenty-eight minutes being used here.

The Sarah Bush Lincoln Heath Center bill stated, Cardarone 150 mg x 2 = $353. which was administered at 12:53

Dex 5% water PF 100/300 IV solution = $49, the paramedics started the IV at the scene.

Cerv (1 view) Radiology = $53, Lateral C-spine X ray was done at 12:47.

Code Blue charge = $510, the Code Blue report is from 12:37 until 1:05 and the paramedics admittance time inside the hospital was at 12:31. I can only assume the Code Blue charge is from the Sarah Bush Lincoln Health Center because the paramedics were done.

Critical Care ER Catego = $993 which the risk manager explained that was customary charges for nursing and other ancillary care provided during the period James was being attended to in their emergency room department. So under what category does the paramedics' actions and their bill falls under?

The coroner is summoned the Sarah Bush Lincoln Health Center to tend to the death of a hanging victim. I asked the coroner what marks he saw on James' neck over the phone and in writing. He said, in writing, that there was a mark beneath the chin. The coroner had the body transported to the pathologist in Springfield, where for the past fifty years they have cremated everything. He knew all incriminating evidence would be gotten rid of. The coroner then held his inquest proceedings with seven jurors who were probably all of the town's people. The investigating officer was friends with the jail staff and could "assure the family there was no foul play involved." The coroner had an all-star cast, so let the show begin. They all worked together for a unanimous suicide verdict. It's signed, sealed, and delivered on James death certificate.

To finalize everything, I paid $975 for an independent conclusion, and they jumped on the bandwagon with the opposition. They boldly and strongly said the asphyxiation by hanging was by suicidal intent. Now they had no organs, no tissues, no brain, and no blood.

On November 9, when the independent pathologist re-opened James' body and saw there was nothing there, he called us because he was concerned. He asked if James had been sick. There are two signatures on the re-autopsy report, and I don't know which pathologist I talked to on November 9. They made a U-turn and went the opposite direction. Little did they know, none of the individuals initially involved with James' body could identify any marks on his neck. Every one officially documented a mark on the chin, underneath the chin. I know they all can distinguish between the chin and the neck, but the independent pathologists wanted to be heroes. They changed the entire game by moving the mark from the chin to the upper lateral portion of the neck.

So we have the jail staff, the Toledo emergency medical team, the Sarah Bush Lincoln Health Center staff, the coroner, the Springfield pathologist, the investigating officer, and the independent pathologists. Okay, challenge all of them, if you want. It is not looking good for James Dawson right about now. The independent pathologists probably talked to our attorney and told him that the asphyxiation by hanging was by suicidal intent because I could not understand why, after four months, he decided they did not have enough evidence to start an investigation. That is also probably why our attorney told us the photographs we had given him showing no marks on James' neck would not be admissible and suggested we try to obtain the official photographs from the coroner's office. The independent pathologists did nothing but add fuel to the fire. Where are my pathologists and crime scene investigators from *Law and Order* and *CSI Miami*? On a brighter note, if we had not requested an independent autopsy, we would have never known James' body was returned to us an empty cavity. If I was Attorney Hopson, and the independent pathologists had revealed this information to me, I think I might have jumped ship, too. Every attorney I came in contact with after Attorney Hopson was more interested in their retainer fees and if I would be able to afford the expenses it would take to investigate a wrongful death claim than all of the unusual and suspicious circumstances surrounding my brother's death. Now I understand why people don't attempt to fight for justice or give up in their fight.

We must look beyond the suicide allegation. We must dissect what is being presented. Once people read this documentary, I know everyone will suspect wrongdoing because there are just too many inconsistencies. It is unfortunate I had to encounter individuals who did not want to waste time investigating our wrongful death claim. It was easier not to get involved. Look at all of the individuals they would have had to challenge. Who needs this headache? Regardless of their reason for not assisting us in our fight for justice, I have no other choice but to accept it. However, when the Lord steps in and puts his hands on the situation, it's a new ball game. It's the bottom of the ninth, and the score is tied, with the Lord at bat. Look out; this ball game is over, and that is how I was able to compile and write this documentary.

We all know something went terribly wrong on November 5, 2000, when James was taken inside the Cumberland County jail. We may never know what really happened because the only person who can tell us has been silenced forever. I speak from the grave of that silenced voice and others before him, and unfortunately, those that will come after him. I want you to hear their scream. "I did not take my own life." I want you to see just how easy it is to put a suicide label on anyone. I want you to see how easy it is to steal organs and to get rid of evidence. Know your gut feelings, know what your loved ones are made of, and know that this, too, could happen to you.

This documentary is the evidence in the wrongful death claim for James Dawson. Due to the fact that we were denied legal assistance and the legal assistance we did receive felt we did not have sufficient evidence, I hope this documentary is sufficient. After reading this documentary and no evidence is found, at least, I have gotten my brother's story out.

I end my story by first thanking God for allowing James' breath to be placed inside me so that I could deliver his story. I thank God for my outstanding cast, my mother, brother, and son, for letting me interrogate them and bring out every possible memory. They deserve a standing ovation. I thank God for family, friends, and supporters. I thank God for all who have contributed to our fight for justice. I thank God for Wilson N. Winters, Jr. because without him, mentally and financially, I could not have completed my journey.

Serenity Prayer

GOD GRANT ME THE
SERENITY
TO ACCEPT THE THINGS I CANNOT CHANGE,
COURAGE
TO CHANGE THE THINGS I CAN, AND THE
WISDOM
TO KNOW THE DIFFERENCE.

A SPECIAL TRIBUTE TO MY GRANDMA SARAH:

She supported me throughout my journey. As I watched her battle cancer, she was my hero. I read my documentary to her and told her that one day it will become a book. She smiled and told me how proud she was of me. She never complained and always thanked God every day. She never went a day without telling her loved ones that she loved them. I was blessed to be with my grandmother on July 7, 2009 when she took her last breath. She opened her eyes, shed a tear, and then she was gone. There is a joyous celebration for grandma and James.

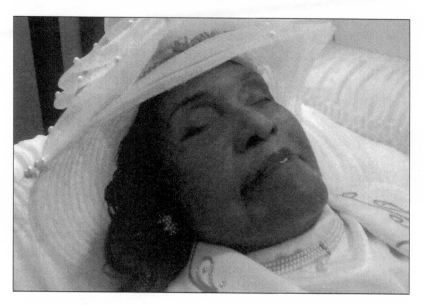

I love you grandma!

Author: Margaret (Dawson) Brown

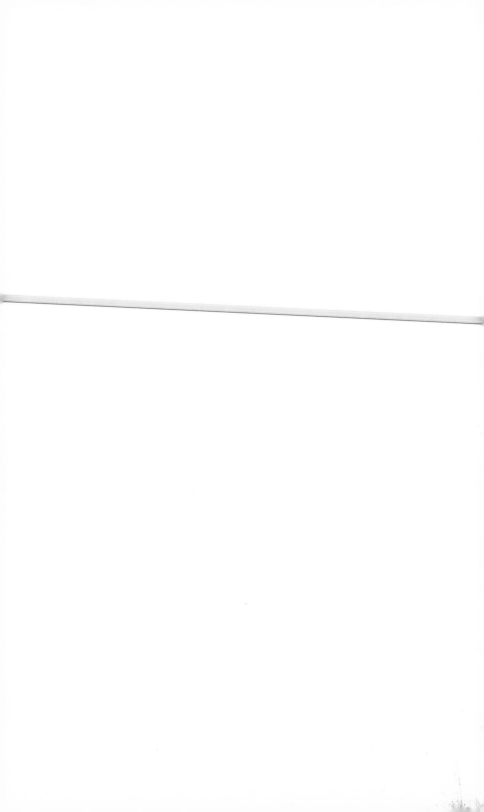

87078257R00128

Made in the USA
Lexington, KY
19 April 2018